DIVINE COUNTDOWN

God's Prophetic Timeline

Sherri L. Reynolds

Footprint Publications

Copyright © 2024 Sherri L. Reynolds

Second Edition August 2024

All rights reserved. No part of this publication may be reproduced, distributed, or transmitted in any form or by any means, including photocopying, recording, or other electronic or mechanical methods, without the prior written permission of the publisher, except in the case of brief quotations embodied in critical reviews and certain other noncommercial uses permitted by copyright law. For permission requests, contact Footprint Publications at **footprintpublishing@gmail.com**
Disclaimer: Under Section 107 of the Copyright Act 1976, allowance is made for "fair use" for purposes such as criticism, comment, news reporting, teaching, scholarship, and research. Fair use is a use permitted by the copyright statute that might otherwise be infringing.

ISBN - 9798323710928

DEDICATION

I would like to dedicate my work to those I hold dearest on this earth. First, to my husband, Jim, who lovingly supports me and has afforded me the many hours to complete this study. Then to my kids, Ashley and Brandon, who bring joy to my life and are my inspiration to pass on a Godly heritage. Next, to my mother, Lonnie Memmer, who made sure I had a Godly foundation from an early age and has lived out her life's motto, "Overcomer". Lastly, in memory of my father, Fred Memmer, the mentor, and earthly pillar of my faith, who showed me a life and legacy worthy of emulating.

SPECIAL THANKS

I am grateful to God for His sovereign hand in my life. I will never take for granted the Godly home He placed me in at birth, the church I was raised in, the Christian high school and University I attended, and the desire in me to study, learn, and grow. I am glad for the little that I can give back to Him for the unspeakable gift of eternal life that He has given me. I would also like to thank the late prophecy author and teacher, Ted Naman. His knowledge, input, edits, and encouragement were invaluable to me in this process. Thirdly, I would like to thank my longtime friend and publisher David Michael Lee who spent long hours making this book a reality, coaching me, and letting me in on the "frustratingly, addictive fun". I would also like to thank my husband, Jim, for his constant support, encouragement, and motivation to make this happen. His contributions were vital in helping me to reach this goal. Whenever there is a project, we have always made a great team. Lastly, to my son, Brandon, for his time and creativity in the book title and cover design.

Preface

Do you really want to understand what the Bible has to say about end times but just feel too intimidated to dive into Revelation, Ezekiel, and Daniel? I have attended several end time studies in my life, and often more seats had to be brought in. We are all eager to know what our future holds.
Fortunately, as a child in my early elementary years, I was taught the basics of the end times. My parents attended a home Bible study where their Sunday school teacher, Carl Brooks, spent weeks laying out charts and explaining in detail what the Bible had to say about end times. The plan was for my sister and I to sit quietly on the carpet of the living room off to the side finishing homework or coloring while the adults engaged in the end times study.

Sitting there on the floor, I was captivated immediately, and I never touched the things I had brought to occupy me during those studies. The sound Biblical foundation that I gained in second grade was invaluable to me through the years. It was a foundation that I have built on and found deep security in, knowing that an all-powerful sovereign God had all past history, present events, and future plans in His hands.

As a mother of two, I wanted that same assurance, peace, and security for my high school aged kids. So, I made it my mission to type out a chronological outline, complete with timelines, charts, and pictures, and incorporating current events, in an effort to pass my knowledge on to my kids.
In many cases, I could not find the charts that I was looking for on the internet, so I created timelines and charts myself in an attempt to make the material as understandable as possible.

The reason this material is in bullet point form and not narrative is because I was teaching it to my kids and not reading it to them. I wanted to be looking at them and interacting with them instead of having my head down with my nose in a book.

We took our time getting through the material, but I am happy to report that we made it all the way through. As people began to find out that I had done this, they wanted a copy of my work for themselves. I was encouraged to combine all my charts and pictures into one document, making it easier to send out electronically. I was also encouraged to publish my work.

I am grateful to my husband, Jim Reynolds, prophecy author and teacher Ted Naman, and my publisher David M. Lee for encouraging me in this effort. I pray that these pages will be inspirational to those who read them and that ultimately, they will encourage you to draw closer to the Savior and Lord Who gave His life that we may enjoy the amazing eternity He is preparing for those who believe on His name.

Table of Contents

Dedication and Special Thanks — 4
Preface — 5
Before You Begin Reading — 9

Chapter 1 - God's Timeline — 11
   Definition of Biblical Prophecy — 12
   Reasons to Know Bible Prophecy — 12
   Biblical Timeline — 14
   Chart: Timeline from Eternity Past to Eternity Future — 16

Chapter 2 – Israel's History — 17
   Jewish/ Islamic History — 18
      Ancient History — 18
      Illustration: Original Land God Promised Israel — 19
   Jewish History from the Kings to Modern History — 20
      Illustration: Destruction of Jerusalem AD 70 — 21
   Modern History — 23
      Illustration: Map of Israel — 24
      Illustration: Who Occupies Israel — 25
      Illustration: Modern History Timeline — 25
   Israel Currently — 26
      Understanding Israel's Place of Importance — 26
      Battle for Temple Mount — 27
      Illustration: Current Day Temple Mount — 27
      Temple Preparations — 27
      Theories – Where is the Ark? — 28

Chapter 3 – The World's Role — 29
   Current World Factors that Lead to End Times War — 30
      Oil Supply — 30
      Illustration: 12 Tribes Land Division — 30
      Islamic Factor — 31
      European Union — 32
   America's Role in Bible Prophecy — 33
      History — 33
      Three Takes on America's Role in Prophecy — 34
      Birth Pains of the End Times — 35

Chapter 4 – Imminent Rapture
- Imminent Rapture — 37
  - Times of the Gentiles — 38
  - Chart: Nebuchadnezzar's Dream of an Image — 38
  - Seven Churches of Revelation — 39
  - Chart: The Church Age — 40
  - Customs of the Galilean Wedding — 41
  - Seven Annual Jewish Feasts — 42
  - Chart: Seven Annual Feasts of Israel — 43
  - — 44

Chapter 5 – The Rapture — 45
- Rapture — 46
  - Signs that the Second Coming (not the Rapture) is Near — 46
  - Chart: From the Cross to Eternity — 47
  - Order of the Rapture — 48

Chapter 6 – The Tribulation — 51
- Tribulation Defined — 52
- Tribulation Purpose — 52
- Chart: The Tribulation — 53
- Will Christians Go Through the Tribulation? — 53

Chapter 7 – What Happens in Heaven During the Tribulation — 57
- What Will Happen in Heaven During the Tribulation — 58
  - Bema Seat Judgement — 58
  - Crowns Earned — 58
  - Good Works With Good Motives — 59
  - Good Works With Wrong Motives — 60
  - Attitude of a Christian Toward This Judgement — 60
  - Results of the Bema Seat — 60
  - After the Bema Seat — 61
  - War in Heaven at the Midpoint of the Tribulation — 61
  - Marriage of the Lamb — 61
  - Marriage Supper of The Lamb — 61

Chapter 8 – What Happens on Earth – First 3 ½ Years — 63
- What Happens on Earth During the Tribulation? — 64
  - Immediately After the Rapture — 64
  - Battle of Gog and Magog — 65
  - First 3 ½ Years of the Tribulation — 67
  - Chart: Tribulation Events — 69
  - The Seven Seal Judgements — 70
  - Chart: The Seven Seals of Revelation — 73

Seven Trumpet Judgements	74
Chart: The Seven Trumpets of Revelation	76
Seven Key Figures	77
Chart: Seven Figures of Revelation	79
Midpoint of the Tribulation	80
Chapter 9 – What Happens on Earth – Last 3 ½ Years	**83**
Last 3 ½ Years of the Tribulation	84
Seven Bowl Judgements	85
Chart: The Seven Bowls of Revelation	86
Dooms of Babylon	87
Chapter 10 – The Second Coming of Christ	**89**
The Second Coming of Christ	90
Description of the Lord at His Second Coming	90
Returning with Armies of Christ	91
Physical Changes	91
Reshaping of Jerusalem	91
The Avenging Christ	91
Armageddon	92
After Armageddon	93
75-day interval	94
Chapter 11 – The Millennium	**95**
The Millennium	96
Characteristics	97
Different Millennial Views	99
End of the Millennium	100
Great White Throne Judgement	100
Books Opened	101
After the Great White Throne Judgement	102
Chapter 12 – The Eternal State	**103**
New Heaven, Earth, and Jerusalem	104
New Jerusalem	104
Characteristics of the Eternal State	105
Response to the Knowledge	106
References	**108**
About the Author	**109**

Before You Begin Reading

I wrote this study from the perspective that I and both of my kids have made a profession of faith in Jesus Christ as our Lord and Savior. With our future sealed and secure in the hand of God, scripture tells us that we are saved from the wrath of God to come (Rom 5:9). We will not see the devastation this sinful world will endure. We will be safe with our Savior. If you are not sure and completely confident of your future, please read the following.

First, we need to acknowledge the fact that every human ever born is a sinner. God is holy and has given us a standard which we have all failed to live up to (Rom 3:23). Since no human is capable of obeying God's law perfectly, we are all condemned to death, not only physical death, but also spiritual death, which is an eternity apart from the God Who created us, to pay the penalty of our sin ourselves (Rom 6:23).

Second, we need to acknowledge the fact that God loved us so much that He provided a way to save man from this eternal punishment (John 3:16). He sent His only Son, Jesus Christ, to earth in human form to live a perfect, sinless life and then willingly take the sin of the world upon Himself and offer Himself as a sacrifice, paying the penalty of sin for all mankind (Heb 10:10). He then rose from the dead (I Cor 15:3-4), conquering the penalty of death (I Cor 15:54-57), and ascended back to His Father in heaven (Heb 10:12). Jesus Christ is the only One who is capable of forgiving us. He is the only way to a right relationship to our God and Creator (John 14:6).

Third, we need to acknowledge the fact that Jesus Christ is offering us a gift (Eph 2:8-9). That gift is the gift of atonement, Christ's payment of our sin by death on the cross, in exchange for our holiness in the eyes of God (Heb 12:14). He has paid the price of death for us and in exchange He is offering us the gift of forgiveness and eternal life (Acts 26:18). If we accept the gift, we are in right standing with the Creator of the universe (Rom 5:19). If we reject it, we are left to pay the price of eternal death ourselves (Rom 6:23).

Fourth, we need to acknowledge the fact that we are responsible and accountable for the choice we make. No one can make the decision for us and no one else will receive the rewards or punishment for this decision we have made (Rom 14:10-12).

Fifth, receiving the gift is a very simple process. All you need to do is confess with your mouth the Lord Jesus and believe in your heart that God has raised Him from the dead. The Word of God says if you do this, you will be saved (Rom 10:9). We are saved presently from the power of sin in our lives, and we are saved in the future from the wrath of God to come (Rom 5:9). We are His child, and He will love us as His own. We are a member of His family and we become an heir to all things He has given His Son (Rom 8:14-17).

Sixth, if you have made the choice to accept this gift, you should live a life that shows your gratefulness and obedience to God (Col 1:10-12). You do this by joining those of like faith as a team (I Cor 12:12-13, Heb 10:25), seeking to deepen your relationship to God by spending time in the Bible and praying, and finding ways to serve Him while you are on this earth (Col 1:10).

Lastly, as a child of God, He encourages us to look forward to His appearing (II Tim 4:8). We are to take courage knowing that our future is secured (Eph 1:13), and that one day we will see the One Who saved us face to face (I Cor 13:12). He promised that He is currently preparing a place for us (John 14:2-4). What a place it will be!!

If you have just made this decision, I want to personally welcome you to the family of God. I would like to encourage you to find a body of believers who base their faith in the Bible alone. Get plugged in. Grow your faith and relationship with God. Read His Word, spend time with Him in prayer, and find a place to serve Him out of love for what He has done for you. I would also encourage you to enjoy the assurance you now have that God has your future. You are rescued from His wrath to come, and you are destined for an eternal life of peace with God.

Sherri

CHAPTER 1

GOD'S TIMELINE

Definition of Biblical Prophecy

- **Prophecy is a prediction or a forecast of <u>future</u> events.**
- **Biblical prophecy is a prediction or forecast of future events according to <u>God's</u> written revelation.**
  - God spoke these words to <u>chosen</u> men who is turn wrote them down – II Pet 1:20-21.
  - These words are recorded in the <u>66</u> books of the Bible.
- **There are <u>two</u> categories of Biblical prophecy.**
  - Foretold events which have already happened with <u>100%</u> accuracy.
  - Foretold events which have <u>yet</u> to take place.
- **This study is a focus of foretold Biblical events which have yet to take place and the <u>history</u> behind their significance.**

Reasons to Know Bible Prophecy

- **Prophecy reveals the most important subject of the ages: God's plan for <u>man</u>.**
  - Man is God's most <u>prized</u> creation.
  - It shows His never-ending <u>pursuit</u> of man, His longsuffering for the sinner, to what lengths He will go to rescue man, and reward for those who choose Him.
  - Prophecy gives us a glimpse into God's bountiful plans for the <u>future</u> of those who believe in Him and obey His word – Jer 29:11.
- **Prophecy convinces us that there really is a <u>God</u>.**
  - All of God's past prophecies have been fulfilled which gives us complete <u>confidence</u> that the future prophecies will be fulfilled as well.
  - If the over <u>300</u> OT prophecies were perfectly fulfilled concerning the birth of Christ, then the over <u>1,845</u> prophecies concerning the end times will be perfectly fulfilled as well.
- **Prophecy prepares the believer to recognize and avoid the deception of <u>false</u> teaching.**
  - False teachings can come in the form of false faiths, false worldviews, and false <u>cultural thinking</u>.
  - If we learn and know the <u>truth</u> from God's word, we will not be deceived or be drawn away into worldly thinking.
- **Prophecy tends to purify and <u>motivate</u> the believer.**
  - When we understand the prophecies of the end times, it motivates us to live more <u>holy</u> lives so we will not be surprised or ashamed at His second coming.
  - When we realize that our works and rewards do <u>follow</u> us into eternity, we will prioritize our lives accordingly and strive for the rewards – Rev 14:13.
- **Prophecy heightens our <u>compassion</u> for others and their need to know the truth.**
  - There is no other more important <u>message</u> to get out.

- - We will devote our lives to living out and sharing God's <u>gift</u>. It will become a priority in our decision making.
  - <u>Partner</u> with God and pull as many as you can from the claws of Satan.
- **Prophecy offers confident <u>hope</u> in a hopeless age.**
  - Things can tend to look dismal. If we focus on the news, hopelessness and depression can set in. It can even paralyze us spiritually and emotionally but, as the saying goes, "I read the back of the book, and we <u>win</u>".
  - When we know the outcome, we have the drive to fight. It should actually <u>energize</u> us. If we are fighting on God's side, then let's fight well and fight hard.
- Our time is <u>short</u> (which we will see).
- We need to be prepared. <u>Knowing</u> prepares.
- It was not written to scare us but to guide and <u>prepare</u> us for God's future eternity.
- It is a <u>wake-up</u> call!!

NOTES:

Biblical Timeline

Overview from eternity past to eternity future (main events of history – His Story)

- **Creation** – 4004 BC
  - Creation of Adam and Eve (<u>sinless</u> perfection) – Gen 1:1-2:25.
- **Fall of man**
  - Into disobedience and <u>sin</u>– Gen 3:1-24.
  - Need for and promise of a <u>Savior</u> – Gen 3:15.
- **Flood** – 2350 BC
  - The Lord observed the extent of human <u>wickedness</u> on the earth, and He saw that everything they thought or imagined was constantly and totally evil – Gen 6:5.
  - The Lord was <u>sorry</u> He ever made them and put them on the earth – Gen 6:6.
  - It broke His heart, and He started over with <u>Noah</u> – Gen 6:7-9:19.
- **Babel** – 2247 BC
  - Man's disobedience to God culminated in establishing their own <u>religion</u> – Gen 11:1-4.
  - They erected a tower in honor and worship of <u>man</u> – Gen 11:4.
  - God confused the languages, and the people <u>scattered</u> – Gen 11:6-9.
- **Abraham** – 1921 BC (year of his calling).
  - Call of Abraham from <u>Ur</u> to the Promised Land – Gen 12:1-3; Acts 7:2-4.
  - He is the father of the nation of <u>Israel</u> (Gen 12:2) and is given the promise of a Savior through his son Isaac - Gen 17:19.
  - Their family became known as the <u>Hebrews</u> – Gen 14:13.
  - It was at this time that God, the Creator, gave the land of Israel to Abraham and his descendants through <u>Isaac's</u> line – Gen 12:1,7;13:14-17: 15:18-21; 17:8,19.
- **Isaac** – 1900 BC
  - Abraham's son from <u>Sarah</u> – Gen 21:1-3.
  - He was the promised son and <u>heir</u> – Gen 17:19.
  - God confirmed His covenant and promise to <u>Isaac</u> – Gen 26:2-4.
- **Jacob** – 1765 BC
  - God confirmed His covenant and promise to <u>Jacob</u> – Gen 28:13-15.
  - His name was changed to Israel when he <u>wrestled</u> with God – Gen 32:24-28.
  - He had twelve sons which formed the 12 <u>tribes</u> of Israel – Gen 49:1-18.
- **Egypt** – 1706 BC
  - Israelites were enslaved for <u>400</u> years – Gen 15:13-14; Ex 1:7-22.
- **Moses** – 1491 BC
  - Brought the Israelites out of slavery from <u>Egypt</u> – Ex 2:1-14:31.
  - The <u>Law</u> was given (10 Commandments) – Ex 19:1-23:33.

- o God gave Moses specific instructions on building the <u>Tabernacle</u> – Ex 24:1-30:10.
- **Judges** – 1400 BC
  - o After they were established in the Promised Land, <u>judges</u> ruled the nation of Israel – Judges 1:1-21:25.
- **Kings** – 1050 BC
  - o Israelites demanded a <u>king</u> – I Sam 8:1-22.
  - o Kings ruled Israel for many years. Saul, David, and Solomon were the <u>first</u> three kings – I Sam 9:1-II Chron 36:23.
  - o The tabernacle was replaced by a permanent <u>Temple</u> during Solomon's reign – I Kings 6:37-38.
  - o Israel <u>divided</u> into a Northern kingdom (Israel) and a Southern kingdom (Judah) – I Kings 12:16-33.
- **Captivity** – 650 BC
  - o Because of their <u>disobedience</u> and idolatry, the nation of Israel was taken into captivity – Deut 29:26-28; Ez 39:23-24.
  - o Israel was taken captive by Assyria (II Kings 17:4-23) and Judah by <u>Babylon</u> – II Kings 24:10-25:30.
- **Israel** – Free again – 536 BC
  - o The Persian emperor <u>Cyrus</u> the Great, allowed the Israelites to return to their homeland to rebuild the Temple in Jerusalem – II Chron 36:22-23.
- **Jesus** – AD 33
  - o <u>Promised</u> Savior – Birth/life/death/burial/resurrection/ascension of Christ – Matt, Mark, Luke, John.
- **Church Age**
  - o <u>Pentecost</u> (AD 33) until the Rapture – Acts 2:1-4.
- **Jerusalem** – AD 70
  - o The city was <u>destroyed</u> by the Romans under Titus – Matt 24:2.
  - o The Jewish people were <u>dispersed</u> into other nations around the world – Ez 12:15; 34:5.
- **Israel granted statehood.**
  - o May 14, <u>1948</u> – Ez 36:24.
- **Rapture** – I Thess 4:13-18.
- **Tribulation** – Dan 9:27.
- **Second Coming** – Rev 19:11-16.
- **Armageddon** – Rev 16:12-16; 19:17-19.
- **Millennium** – Rev 20:4.
- **New heaven and new earth** – Rev 21:1-22:5.

Where are we on the timeline now? – <u>End</u> of the Church Age.

What is the Next Event on God's timeline? – The <u>Rapture</u>.

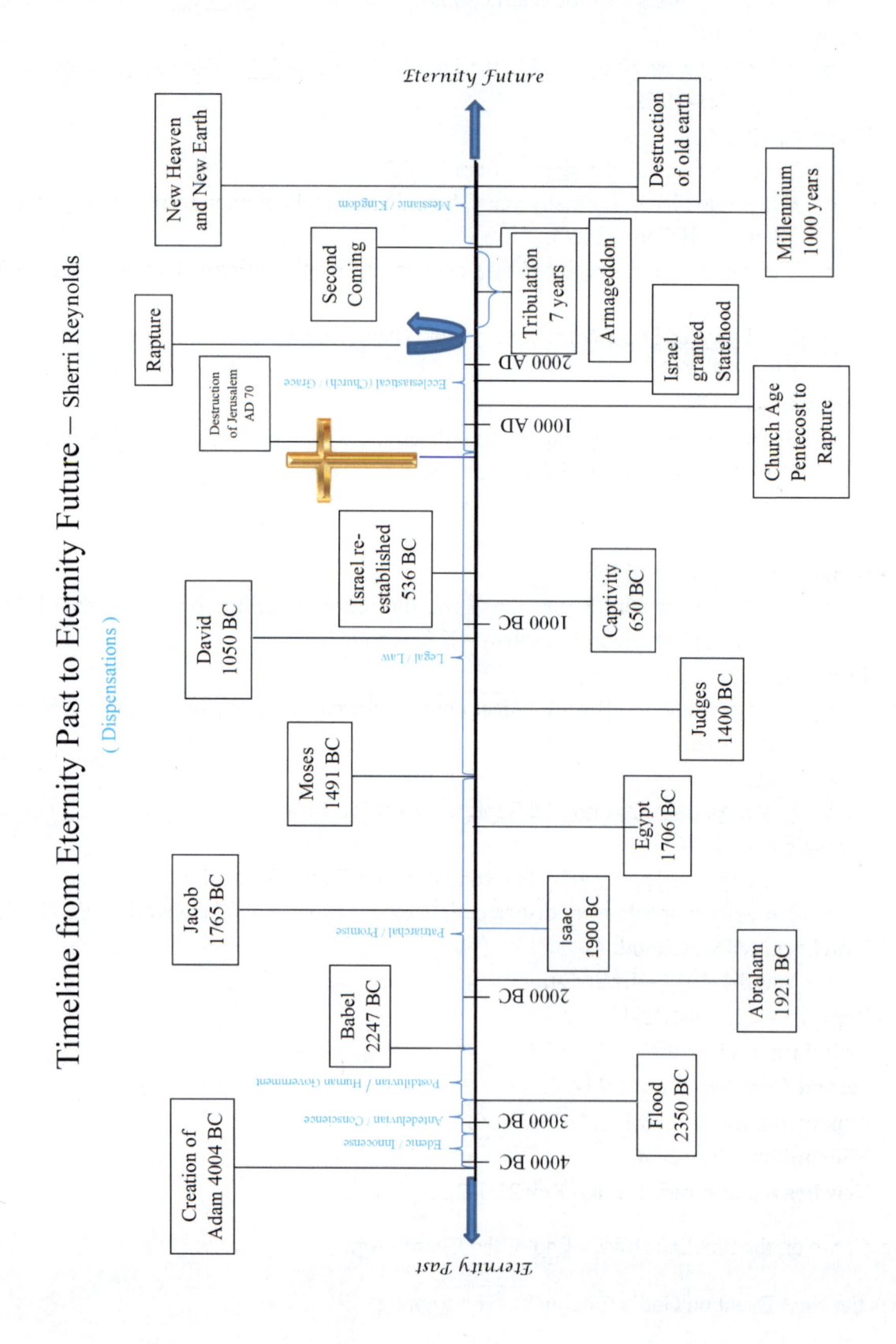

Timeline from Eternity Past to Eternity Future — Sherri Reynolds

(Dispensations)

Eternity Past → **Eternity Future**

- Creation of Adam 4004 BC
- Edenic / Innocence
- 4000 BC
- Antediluvian / Conscience
- 3000 BC
- Flood 2350 BC
- Postdiluvian / Human Government
- Babel 2247 BC
- 2000 BC
- Abraham 1921 BC
- Isaac 1900 BC
- Patriarchal / Promise
- Jacob 1765 BC
- Egypt 1706 BC
- Moses 1491 BC
- Judges 1400 BC
- Legal / Law
- David 1050 BC
- 1000 BC
- Captivity 650 BC
- Israel re-established 536 BC
- ✝ (Cross)
- Destruction of Jerusalem AD 70
- Ecclesiastical (Church) / Grace
- 1000 AD
- Church Age Pentecost to Rapture
- 2000 AD
- Israel granted Statehood
- Rapture
- Tribulation 7 years
- Armageddon
- Second Coming
- Millennium 1000 years
- Messianic / Kingdom
- Destruction of old earth
- New Heaven and New Earth

CHAPTER 2

ISRAEL'S HISTORY

Jewish/Islamic History

Ancient History

- God called for Himself a <u>people</u> – Deut 7:6.
    - To make His <u>Name</u> known – Ez 39:7.
        - At the second coming of Christ, He has a <u>new</u> name that no one knows – Rev 19:12.
        - This name will never have been taken in vain.
    - To make them a blessing to the <u>nations</u> (Savior would come from this people) – Gen 12:3.
- Abraham was promised a son and a <u>land</u>. Son – Gen 15:4-5. Land – Gen 15:18.
- <u>Both</u> religions claim Abraham as their founding father.
    - Jews through Abraham's son <u>Isaac</u> (Sarah). The covenant was established through Isaac – Gen 17:19.
    - Islam through Abraham's son <u>Ishmael</u> (Hagar), Ishmael did become a great nation – Gen 17:20.
- God confirms His promise through Isaac (Gen 26:3-4) and then <u>Jacob</u> (Gen 28:11-22, renamed Israel – Gen 35:10, father of the 12 tribes – Gen 49:3-28).
- Slavery in <u>Egypt</u> for 400 years – Gen 15:13.
- <u>Moses</u> leads them back to the Promised Land – Ex 3 - Josh 1.
    - Tabernacle (mobile version of the Temple – Ex 24:1-30:10) which is the focal point of worship of the One True God on earth, place of <u>significance</u> during the Tribulation (Dan 9:27) and the Millennium – Ez 40-46; Rev 20:6.
- <u>Original</u> boundaries of The Promised Land – Gen 15:18-21, Num 34:3-12, Ez 48:1-29.
    - North – at Hamath – 100 miles North of <u>Damascus</u> – Ez 48:1.
    - Northwest – <u>Mediterranean</u> Sea – Num 34:6.
    - Southwest – <u>Nile River</u> – Gen 15:18.
    - South – Kadesh – 100 miles south of <u>Jerusalem</u> – Ez 48:28.
    - East – <u>Euphrates</u> River – Gen 15:18.
    - This would include Lebanon, <u>West Bank</u> of Jordan, Syria, Iraq, and Saudi Arabia.
- Judges ruled – Judges 1:1-21:25.

Original Land God Promised Israel

Jewish History from the Kings to Modern History

- **Kings Ruled** – Saul/David/Solomon
    - Solomon built the Temple, permanent dwelling place of God on earth during this time of Israel's history – I Kings 6:1-38.
- **586 BC**
    - Jerusalem fell to Nebuchadnezzar, king of Babylon (Iraq) – II Kings 24:10-25:30.
    - Temple destroyed – II Chron 36:7, Jer 34:1-3, Dan 1:1-7.
- **538 BC**
    - Under Cyrus the Great, they let Jews return to Jerusalem – II Chron 36:22-23.
    - Temple was rebuilt –Ezra 5:13-16.
- **400 BC**
    - Close of OT, Greeks ruled Jerusalem.
- **4 BC**
    - Opening of the NT, Romans ruled Jerusalem but allowed Jews to practice their own religion – Luke 2:1-3; Matt 2:1.
- **4-6 BC**
    - Jesus was born – Luke 1:26 – 2:20.
- **AD 33**
    - Jesus was crucified under Roman rule – John 19:16-24.
- **AD 33**
    - After Pentecost, the nation of Israel is distinct from The Church – Dan 9:24-26.
    - God's Spirit is in the church, both Jew and Gentile – Col 3:11.
- **AD 70**
    - The nation of Israel rebelled against Roman rule under Titus and Jerusalem was destroyed in AD 70.
    - Jesus predicted that one stone would not be left upon another – Matt 24:2.
    - When the fires destroyed the Temple, all its gold melted and ran between the stone. Every stone was literally picked apart by the Romans for the gold.

Destruction of Jerusalem AD 70

- After the Jews <u>rejected</u> Jesus as their promised Messiah, God set them aside for now to focus on spreading the Gospel among the Gentiles through the preaching and teaching of the apostle Paul and Jesus' disciples – Rom 3:29.
- The church is currently made up of more Gentiles than Jews. Jesus will turn His attention back to the Jewish people <u>after</u> the Rapture of the church during the seven-year tribulation which is Daniel's 70th week (Dan 9:24). 69 weeks are completed, 483 years from decree by Cyrus to rebuild Jerusalem (March 5, 444 BC unto the Messiah March 30, AD 33).

- The church age started in AD 33 which is parenthetical. Daniel's 70th week will be the seven-year Tribulation – Dan 9:27.
- **AD 135**
  - Bar Kokhba rebellion failure resulted in almost total expulsion of Jews from their homeland.
- **AD 640**
  - Romans built a city over the ruins of Jerusalem along with a pagan temple.
  - After the defeat of Bar Kokhba, Roman emperor Hadrain was determined to wipe out the identity of Israel, Judah, and Judea.
  - Until that time, the area had been called the "province of Judea" by the Romans. He renamed it Syria Palestinia, and Jerusalem was renamed "Aelia Capitolina".
- **AD 640 -1090**
  - After the death of their prophet Muhammad, Muslims conquered Palestine.
  - The Mosque of Omar (Dome of the Rock) and the Al-Aqsa Mosque were built on Temple Mount.
- **AD 1099-1291**
  - Latin or Crusader period – European Christians took back The Holy Land from the Muslims who had destroyed some ancient Christian sites including The Tomb of the Holy Sepulcher.
  - They established a Latin kingdom under the Roman church.
- **AD 1187-1517**
  - Saladin called for "jihad" (holy war) and took back The Holy Land and Jerusalem for Islam. In 1219, Saladin's nephew ordered the destruction of Jerusalem's wall.
- **AD 1517-1917**
  - Ottoman Turks took over and rebuilt Jerusalem. It became a Turkish Muslim city.
  - They rebuilt Jerusalem's wall.

NOTES:

Modern History

- **AD 1914-1918**
  - World War I, the Turks lost control of Palestine to the British.
- **AD 1939-1945**
  - As a result of World War II persecution, Jews wanted to return home.
  - Because of British interest in suppressing anti-Semitism and Western Christians knowing the Jews had to be returned to their homeland to fulfill Bible prophecy before The Second Coming of Christ (Ez 36:6-11, Dan 9:27, Matt 24:15-16, II Thess 2:3-4, Rev 11:1-2), there was a huge push for several decades to establish the nation of Israel back in Palestine.
- **AD 1947**
  - The United Nations declared Jerusalem an international city.
- **AD 1948 – May 14**
  - UN officially recognized the State of Israel. President Truman was the deciding vote.
  - Arab armies flooded Israel. Many Israelis died, but Israel defeated them.
  - The Bible predicted the regathering of Israel a second time (Is 11:11-12), becoming a nation in one day (Is 66:8), and that Israel will never be uprooted again – Amos 9:14-15.
  - This regathering is done in unbelief of Christ as the Messiah in preparation of God's judgement on the Jews during the seven-year Tribulation.
  - The regathering of Israel in belief comes at the end of the seven-year tribulation – Jer 31:7-10, 33:16; Ez 11:14-20.
- **AD 1964**
  - Palestine Liberation Organization was founded under the leadership of Yasser Arafat to fight Israel to give up land to Arab controlled Palestine. These fights continue to this day.
- **AD 1967 – Six Day War**
  - Israeli intelligence Agency learned that Arabs, supplied by Russians, were planning to attack Israel. Predawn air and land attacks by Israel were able to take control of the Sinai Peninsula, West Bank, Golan Heights, and Jerusalem, but they were unable to retain Temple Mount.
- **AD 1973**
  - Yon Kippur War between Israel, and Syria, Jordan, and Egypt who were supported by Russia. The war resulted in Israel defeating all three Arab nations.
- **AD 1978**
  - Camp David Accords – Under US President Jimmy Carter, as a result, Israel returned the Sinai Peninsula to Egypt.

- **AD 1993 and 1995**
    - Oslo Accords, under US President Clinton, blackmailed Israel to give up part of the Promised Land for peace (part of Jerusalem). The agreements were drawn up in Washington DC.
- **AD 1998**
    - Under President Clinton, portions of the West Bank and the Gaza Strip went back to the Palestinians.
- **AD 2020 – September 15**
    - "Abraham Accords" – Treaty brokered by President Trump in favor of Israel and peace in the Middle East. Countries that recognized Israel's sovereignty: Bahrain, United Arab Emirates, Moraco, and Sudan.
    - This could potentially be the framework treaty that the antichrist will confirm to start the seven-year Tribulation clock – Dan 9:27.
- **AD 2023**
    - Iran chants "Death to Israel" – coined by leader Ayatollaha Ali Khamenei – Ps 83:4.
- Currently, there are extreme tensions with Israel. It is surrounded by 22 hostile Arab/Islamic states.
- Whoever blesses Israel will be blessed, whoever curses them will be cursed – Gen 12:3.

Maps of Israel and the West Bank

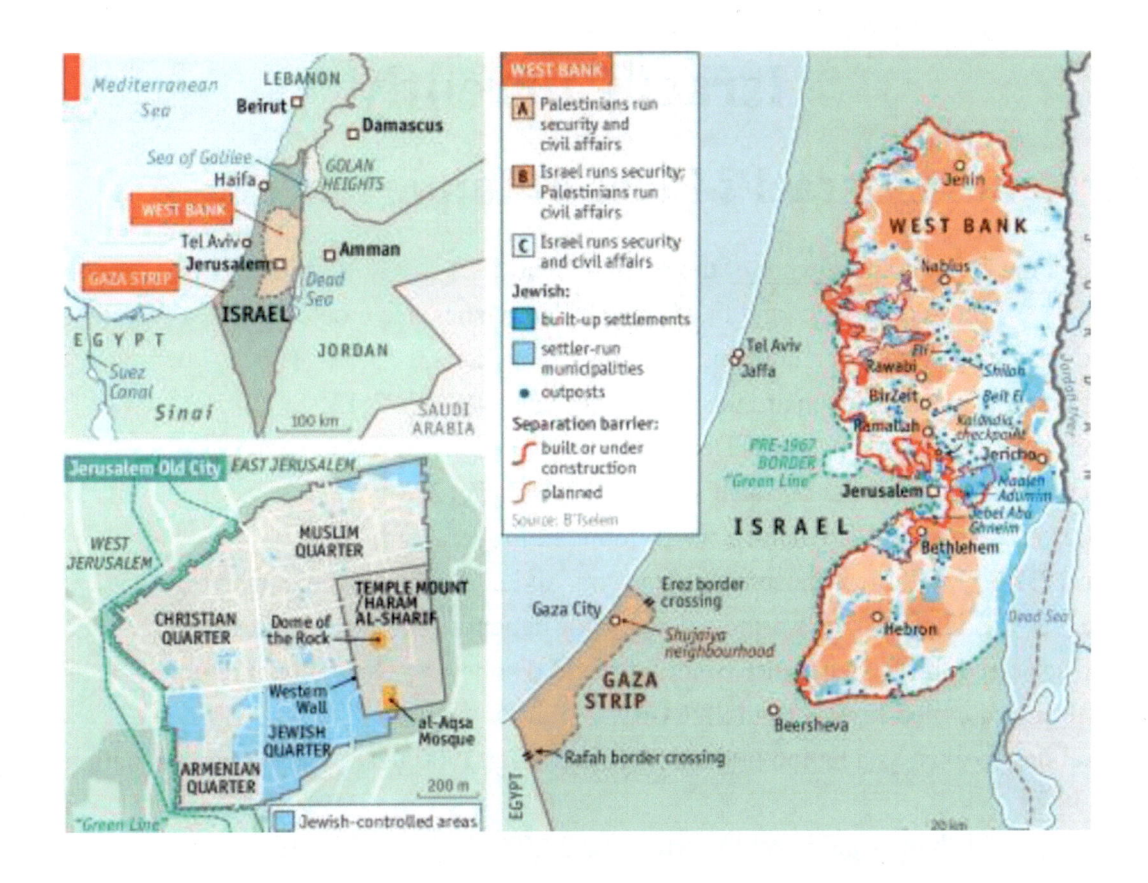

- Mediterranean Sea, Lebanon (Beirut), Damascus, Sea of Galilee, Golan Heights, Haifa, West Bank, Tel Aviv, Jerusalem, Gaza Strip, Dead Sea, Israel, Egypt, Suez Canal, Sinai, Jordan, Saudi Arabia, Amman

Jerusalem Old City / East Jerusalem: West Jerusalem, Christian Quarter, Muslim Quarter, Temple Mount / Haram al-Sharif, Dome of the Rock, Western Wall, Jewish Quarter, al-Aqsa Mosque, Armenian Quarter, "Green Line", Jewish-controlled areas

West Bank legend:
- A — Palestinians run security and civil affairs
- B — Israel runs security; Palestinians run civil affairs
- C — Israel runs security and civil affairs

Jewish: built-up settlements; settler-run municipalities; outposts

Separation barrier: built or under construction; planned

Source: B'Tselem

West Bank locations: Jenin, Nablus, Eli, Rawabi, Shiloh, Birzeit, Beit El, Ramallah, Kalandia checkpoint, Jericho, Jerusalem, Ma'alei Adumim, Jebel Abu Ghneim, Bethlehem, Hebron. Pre-1967 Border "Green Line". Jordan River, Dead Sea.

Gaza Strip: Erez border crossing, Gaza City, Shujaiya neighbourhood, Rafah border crossing, Beersheva, Egypt.

Timeline (50 Years / 50 Years)

	World War II; The Holocaust	"with a stretched out arm, and with fury poured out." Ezekiel 20:33-34
1945	Jews Flee Nazi Persecution	Done for the Lord's namesake, not for Israel's sake. Ezekiel 36:17-24
May 14, 1948	**The Rebirth of Israel**	Reborn in a single day and as one nation, no more two divided kingdoms. Ezekiel 37:16-22; Isaiah 66:7-8
	First Arab-Israeli War	Brought back from the dead to have "an exceedingly great army". Ezekiel 37:1-22
1956	Second Arab-Israeli War	
1967	**Six-Day War; Jews Regain Jerusalem** (Third Arab-Israeli War)	Isa. 11:14
1973	Yom-Kippur War (Fourth Arab-Israeli War)	
1982	First Lebanon War (PLO)	**Wars and Rumors of Wars** "We have heard a voice of trembling, of fear, and not of peace". Jer. 30:5
1987-1993	First Palestinian Intifada	"And ye shall hear of wars and rumors of wars". Matt. 24:6
2000-2005	Second Palestinian Intifada	
2006	Second Lebanon War (Hezbollah)	
2013-	Threats from Russia, Iran, Egypt, Syria, and Turkey	Magog and its allies assemble. Ezek. 38:1-9
2017	**Trump Declares Jerusalem Capital of Israel**	

Israel Currently

Understanding Israel's Place of Importance

- God is the Creator and Owner of the earth – Gen 1:1.
- He has a right to designate land to whomever He wishes. He created it.
- God promised Abraham a land and a nation – Gen 12:1-3, 15:18-21.
- Abraham, Isaac, and Jacob are the fathers of our Faith – Ex 3:15.
- Israel is God's chosen people – Deut 7:6.
- Israel is the nation of the Messiah's origin – II Sam 7:12.
- Judaism, Islam, and Christianity are all founded in Abraham.
- Gen 12:1-3 "I will bless those who bless you, and curse those who curse you".
- The USA had been Israel's principal protector depending on who is president.
- God scattered the Jews because of idolatry and disobeying His commandments – Deut 29:26-28.
- Suffering of exiled Jews – Deut 28:64-67.
- Israel had to exist as a nation in the end times. After 1900 years, they became a nation in 1948 – Ez 36:24.
- Spiritual rebirth of Israel is yet to come – Ez 39:28-29 Deut 4:29-31.

NOTES:

Battle for Temple Mount

- Promise that a third Jewish Temple will be built on Temple Mount– Matt 24:15, II Thess 2:3-4.
    - The Antichrist will desecrate it 3 ½ years into the Tribulation – Dan 9:27.
- Muslim shrines, Dome of the Rock, and Islamic holy place, Al-Aqsa Mosque, on this site currently.
- Depending on the exact location of the original Temple, the Jews could build the third Temple next to the Dome of the Rock. However, the Bible does not tell us where it will be built.

Current Day Temple Mount

Temple Preparations (www.templeinstitute.org)

- A third Temple will be built and in use during the Tribulation.
    - At the midpoint of the Tribulation (3 ½ years), the antichrist will desecrate the Temple by setting himself up as god to be worshipped in it – Dan 9:27, Matt 24:15-16, II Thess 2:3-4, Rev 11:1-2.
- Temple Institute was established in 1987.
- 27,000 Levite priests ready and trained to perform duties.
    - They have been determined to be descendants of Aaron, the first high priest of God.
- Menorah Lampstand, Table of Showbread, red heifer (ashes used in certain purification processes) are all in place.
- Reestablished Sanhedrin ordained in 2004 (70 men, one is selected to be the high priest each year).

- Ark of the Covenant
    - Place where God dwelt on earth between the cherubim – Ex 25:22, Num:7:89, Ps 80:1, Is 37:16.
    - No more power – Ez 8-11. The presence and glory of God departed prior to the Babylonian destruction. It departed in three stages: Ez 10:4, 10:18, 11:22-23. It is seen again in the Millennial temple – Ez 43:1-5.

Theories – Where is the Ark now?

- **Ethiopia – 960 BC.**
    - King Solomon gave it to the Queen of Sheba as a gift which was then handed down through the royal families for protection – I Kings 10:1-13.
    - I cannot see this as a plausible theory because Solomon was the king who built the Temple of God with the Ark as the centerpiece. Why would he have given it away as a gift? – I Kings 6:1-38; 8:1-66.
- **Taken to Egypt by Pharaoh Shishak.**
- **Captured by crusaders and taken to the Vatican in Rome.**
- **Muslims took it to Mecca.**
- **II Chron 35:3** – Prior to the dispersion of the Jews during the Babylonian captivity, King Josiah instructed Levites to "put the Holy Ark in the house", not in the Temple, but where King Solomon had previously prepared to keep the Ark, a "special place, a shelter, in the inward parts".
    - Possibly under the Holy of Holies underneath the Dome of the Rock on Temple Mount, in the City of David, or in another place.
- **Beneath the spot on Golgotha where Jesus was crucified.**
    - Ron Wyatt Jan 6, 1982. Wyatt alleges that he found a series of tunnels and caverns beneath the cross. He found the Ark in a chamber directly under the cross. The ceiling had a crack from the earthquake at Christ's death (Matt 27:51) where the blood of Christ ran down and literally dripped on the Mercy Seat (lid of the Ark) – Lev 16:14-15. He wanted to bring the Ark out but was prevented by an angel saying it was not yet the time.
    - Wyatt had the blood tested. There are a total of 46 chromosomes in human blood, 23 x chromosomes from the mother and 22 x chromosomes and either 1 x or 1 y chromosomes from the father which indicates the gender of a child. This blood had 22 chromosomes identified as a human mother, 1 y chromosome indicating that it was a son, but 22 chromosomes were not humanly identifiable. This indicates that Jesus' Father was God, and that Jesus was truly fully God and fully man.
    - Wyatt Archeological Research – www.wyattmuseum.com

CHAPTER 3

The World's Role

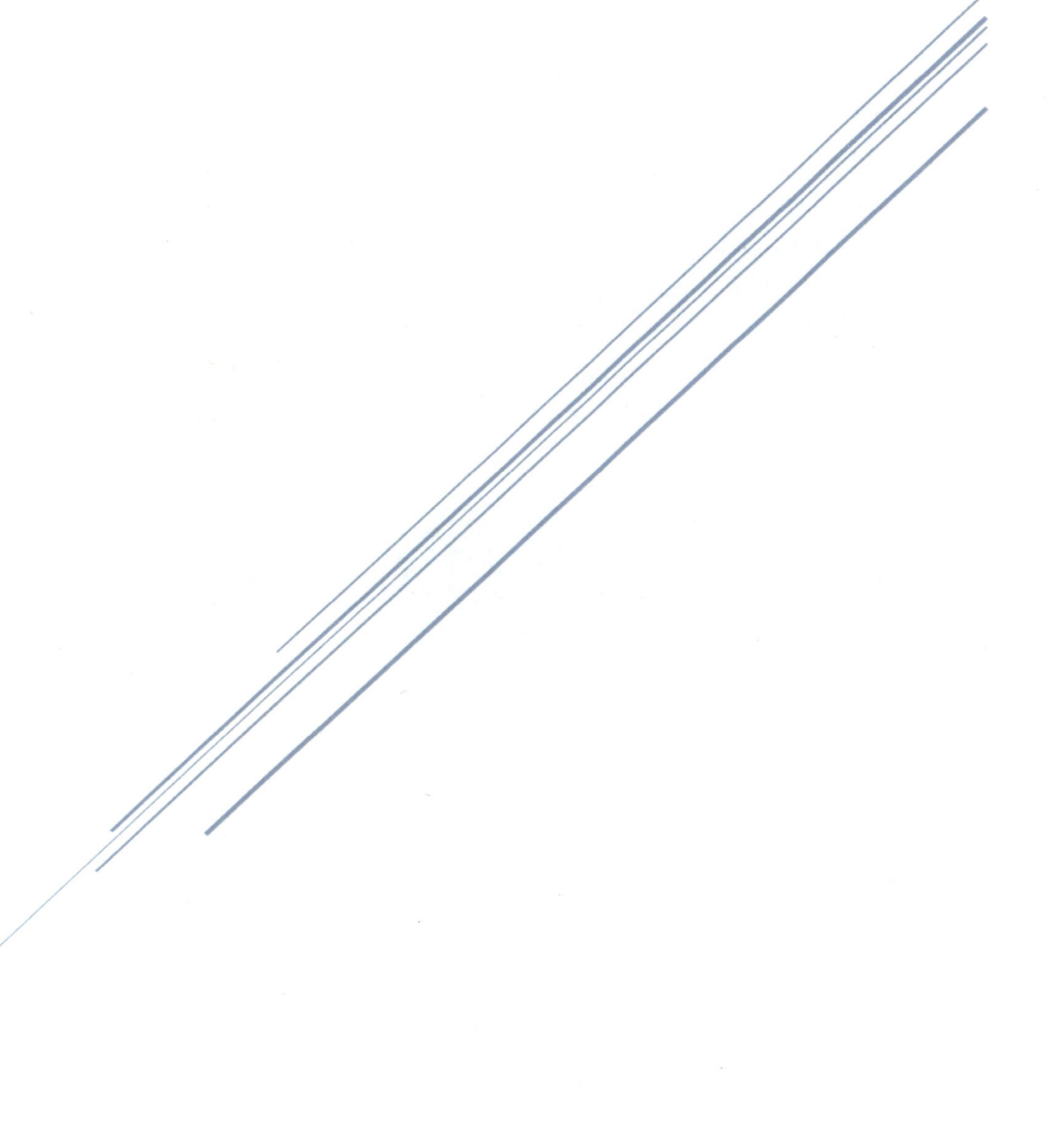

Current World Factors that Lead to End Time War

Oil Supply Factor

- Oil deposits are the result of the decomposition and pressurization of plant and animal life buried by time.
- Some rich deposits are near and around Israel, former region of the Garden of Eden. Potential location, Temple Mount, Gihon spring - Gen 2:10-14, II Chron 32:30, 33:14, Ez 47:1, Rev 22:1.
- Petroleum alliances between Russia and Iran.
- Muslims believe that Allah had entrusted the world's oil supply to them so they can fight against and have victory over Christianized Euro-American civilization.
- Possible shifts of energy power would drastically change world powers.
- Oil is the new gold in the world economy. In 2019, large oil deposits were found in the Mediterranean Sea off the shores of Israel.
- Territory allotted to the twelve tribes.
    - Deut 33:24 – Asher – "foot dipped in oil".
    - Gen 49:22-26 – Joseph – "blessed of the deep that lies beneath".
- Reason for the Gog and Magog war was "to take a spoil" – Ez 38:12-13.

Islamic Factor

- Militant Islamists believe that Jihad (holy war) is the doctrine that Allah has commanded followers to <u>conquer</u> the nations of the world by cultural invasion and by the sword.
- Cultural invasion
    - Moving thousands of Muslim families into a foreign land, build mosques, <u>refuse</u> to assimilate, or adopt that nation's beliefs, and change the culture from the inside out.
    - Move into Europe and America. Have more children than their <u>hosts</u>.
- Their ultimate goal is to conquer the west and America. Radicals teach their children to sing songs of <u>violence</u> and becoming suicide bombers.
- "One day you will see the flag of Islam over the <u>White House</u>" – Muslim activist Anjem Choudary 2010.
- Their goal is political and religious control of the <u>world</u>.
    - Make Islam the <u>religion</u> of public place.
- They await an Islamic Messiah called the Mehdi or the <u>twelfth</u> Imam.
- The hatred that Iran (current name of the Biblical <u>Persia</u>) bears toward the Jewish people will play an important role in a major end time battle – Ez 38-39.
    - There will be an invasion of Israel by a vast coalition of nations all of whom are <u>Islamic</u> today except Russia.
- God and Allah are <u>not</u> the same.

NOTES:

European Union

- The <u>ten</u> toes of Nebuchadnezzar's image represent a 10-kingdom nation from Europe ruled during the Tribulation by the antichrist – Dan 2:41-43.
- EU will be a revived old <u>Roman</u> Empire established after World War II.
- <u>EU</u> will include control of government, religion, and economy.
- 2002 – Monetary unit was established (Euro) to make a common <u>currency</u> between the European nations.
- It will make way for a single chip or <u>mark</u> on hand or forehead – Rev 13:17.
    - With the pandemic, it makes more sense to not have physical money we <u>pass</u> to one another.
- The "harlot woman" of Rev 17 could potentially be the <u>revived</u> Roman Empire, not necessarily the religious system but political, economic, and social.
- Different theories that the "great <u>city</u>" could be Rome, the USA, or a literal Babylon.
- The ten nations will turn against the woman, destroy her, and <u>burn</u> her – Rev 17:16, 18:8.
    - Merchant and kings will <u>mourn</u> her death – Rev 18:9.
    - Ships cannot <u>watch</u> the old literal Babylon burn because it is too far inland – Rev 18:17.
- Her judgement will be swift on <u>one</u> day – Rev 18:17.

NOTES:

America's Role in Bible Prophecy

History

- <u>Columbus</u> lands west of Europe.
  - This land was discovered by Europeans based on a <u>Bible</u> verse – Is 59:19.
- Judeo-Christian <u>heritage</u> of our nation.
  - Our founding fathers wrote the Constitution based on <u>Biblical</u> principles.
- USA <u>friendship</u> with Israel – Gen 12:1-3.
  - God literally promised that He would bless those who bless God's <u>chosen</u> people.
  - It is important that we, as a nation, are <u>pro-Israel</u>.
  - On Dec. 6, 2017, President <u>Trump</u> recognized Jerusalem as the capital and moved the US Embassy back to Jerusalem from Tel Aviv.
  - On Sept. 15, 2020, President <u>Trump</u> signed the Abraham Accords. Trump was the negotiator. Countries that recognized Israel's sovereignty included Bahrain, United Arab Emirates, Moraco, and Sudan.
- USA has been the force behind world <u>missions</u>.
  - By the year 2000, 2/3 of the world's Christians came from countries where western missionaries came from in the <u>1900</u>'s (Lovering, 2012).
  - In the year 2010, the <u>USA</u> sent out 127,000 missionaries, which was over ¼ of the world's 400,000 missionaries (Carter, 2012).

NOTES:

Three Takes on America's Role in Prophecy

- The silence of Scripture on the future of America's role in prophecy is partially since the lands had not yet been <u>discovered</u> when the Bible was written so there would not have been a name for it or its people.
    - It may also indicate that America will have lost her <u>influence</u> either by the time the Tribulation arrives or shortly after and is no longer a major world power.
    - Our Christian heritage is being <u>eroded</u> away and challenged by our culture.
    - <u>Moral</u> decay is setting in and we cannot expect God to bless us as a nation with significant world influence when we have turned out backs on Him.
- The USA will become impotent as a world power because of the Rapture.
    - It could lose millions of its best <u>citizens</u> and therefore, lose its status as a world power.
- Theory that the USA is "Babylon" that falls during the Tribulation (Rev 18) and the nations of the world morn her <u>destruction</u>.
    - It will be eliminated as the world's superpower in a <u>single</u> day by a nationwide nuclear attack which will set the world up that it will easily accept a new global leader (the antichrist).

NOTES:

Birth Pains of the End Times

"For these things must first come to pass" – Luke 21:9.

- Israel's rebirth as a nation, May 14, 1948 – Ez 36:24, Is 11:11-12.
- Plummeting morality since 1960's – II Pet 3:3-4; II Tim 3:1-5, 12-13.
    - As in the days of Noah and Lot – Luke 17:26-30.
        - Noah – wickedness was great and evil continually – Gen 6:5.
        - Lot – cry was great and sin was very grievous – Gen 18:20.
- Famines, violence, rumors of wars and ethnic wars, extreme natural disasters – Matt 24:5-8, Mark 13:7-8, Luke 21:9-11.
- The rise of Russia – her allies are hostile Arab Muslim nations, has a lifelong hostility toward Jews, her outlandish investment in military hardware will be her undoing (Ez 39:9-12), God will destroy her on the mountains of Israel for the purpose of exalting and honoring God among the nations – Ez 38-39.
- Capital and labor conflict and unrest – James 5:1-6.
- Increase in travel and knowledge, age of speed and discovery – Dan 12:4.
- Push for one world government/politics – Dan 2, 7:23.
- Push for one world religion – Rev 13:4, 8, 12.
- Push for one world economy/World Economic Forum – Rev 13:17.
- Rise of political and false religious systems of Babylon – Rev 17.
- Plagues and pestilences – Matt 24:7.
- Covid 19 Pandemic
    - Lockdowns set stage for dictatorship (One leader ruling the world).
    - When people panic, they flock to a leader.
- Calls for government backed cryptocurrency.
    - Paper money is a bacteria spreader.

- Peace treaties with Israel – The treaty is already in place (Potentially the Abraham Accords – Sept. 15, 2020, mediated by President Trump). The antichrist confirms it – Dan 9:27.
- Lukewarm congregation – Rev 3:15-17.
- Apostasy (falling away) from the church – II Tim 3:1-5, I Tim 4:1-4; II Thess 2:3.
- False Christs – Matt 24:4-5.
- False teachers – Col 2:8.
- False prophets – Matt 7:15, 24:11.
- Persecution of believers – Matt 24:9, Luke 21:12-19.

NOTES:

CHAPTER 4

IMMINENT RAPTURE

IMMINENT RAPTURE

There are two depictions in the Bible and two depictions in Jewish culture that show the end times are <u>imminent</u>: Daniels's image in the Old Testament, the seven churches in the New Testament, Galilean wedding customs, and the seven annual Jewish feasts.

Times of the Gentiles
Nebuchadnezzar's dream of an Image (Dan 2:26 – 45)
Gentile World Empires

612-539 BC   **Head of Gold**   **Babylonian Empire**

- Chief deity Murduk – god of gold
- Nebuchadnezzar symbolic of Murduk

539-330 BC   **Chest/Arms of Silver**   **Medo/Persian Empire**

- 2 arms-Dual monarchy

330-63 BC   **Belly/Thighs of Bronze**   **Grecian Empire**

- Phillip Macedon and Alexander the Great

63 BC-AD 1453   **Legs of Iron**   **Roman Empire**

- Empire split in AD 284
- Eastern capitol-Constantinople-fell AD 476
- Western capitol-Rome-fell AD 1453

AD 1453-Present   **Feet of Iron and Clay**   **Divided Roman Empire**

- Racial, Religious, and Political
- Partly strong as iron
- Partly weak as clay

AD Future   **Toes of Iron and Clay**   **Rebirth of Roman Empire**

- European Unification
- European Empire of the last days
- Ten Roman kings

Image crushed by a huge stone – Return of Christ to establish His Millennium kingdom on earth.

Nebuchadnezzar's Dream of an Image

Daniel 2, 7 – Sherri Reynolds

Head of Gold – Dan. 2:32 Lion w/ Eagle's Wings – Dan. 7:4	**Babylonian Empire** 612-539 BC
Breast and Arms of Silver – Dan. 2:32 Bear w/ 3 ribs in	**Medo/Persian Empire** 539-330 BC
Belly & Thighs of Bronze – Dan. 2:32 Leopard w/ 4 wings & 4 heads Dan. 7:6	**Grecian Empire** – 4 divisions of Alexander the Great's kingdom 330-63 BC
Legs of Iron – Dan. 2:33 Beast w/ 10 horns – Dan. 7:7	**Life of Christ** 4 BC – 29 AD **Roman Empire** Eastern & Western 63 BC – AD 1453
Feet of Iron Mingled with Clay Dan. 2:33	**Divided Roman Empire** AD 1453 - Present
Toes of Iron Mingled with Clay Antichrist	**Revived Roman Empire** AD Future

Huge stone crushes the image – Dan. 2:34

Return of Christ - Millennial Kingdom

Seven Churches of Revelation (Rev 2:1-3:19)

AD 30-100	**Ephesus** – Apostolic church, left its first <u>love</u>, preoccupied, backslidden, their deeds became their doctrine.
AD 100-313	**Smyrna** – Roman persecution, chastised by the Lord, <u>death</u>, 10 waves of persecution.
AD 313-600	**Pergamum** – Age of Constantine, Satan's seat, marriage of paganism and Christianity, Roman Catholic church was the established <u>state</u> church, lax.
AD 600-1517	**Thyatira** – <u>Dark</u> ages, "works", Papal (Catholic church), neglectful church.
AD 1517-1648	**Sardis** – Dead church, powerless, resulted in the <u>Reformation</u>.
AD 1648-1900	**Philadelphia** – Missionary movement, Open door, Persevering church, City of earthquakes, <u>pillars</u> were often the only thing left standing – Rev 3:12.
AD 1900-Present	**Laodicea** – Apostasy, <u>lukewarm</u>, Christ-less church, "Lao" – people, "dicea" – rights.

Some Bible scholars believe we are at the end of the <u>Laodicean</u> Church age.
Other scholars believe that we are currently still in the <u>Philadelphia</u> church time period and are now overlapping the Laodicea church. At the Rapture, the Philadelphia church (faithful, true believers) will be caught up and the Laodicea church (apostate, unbelieving church) will be left behind to go through the Tribulation (Rev 3:7-19).

NOTES:

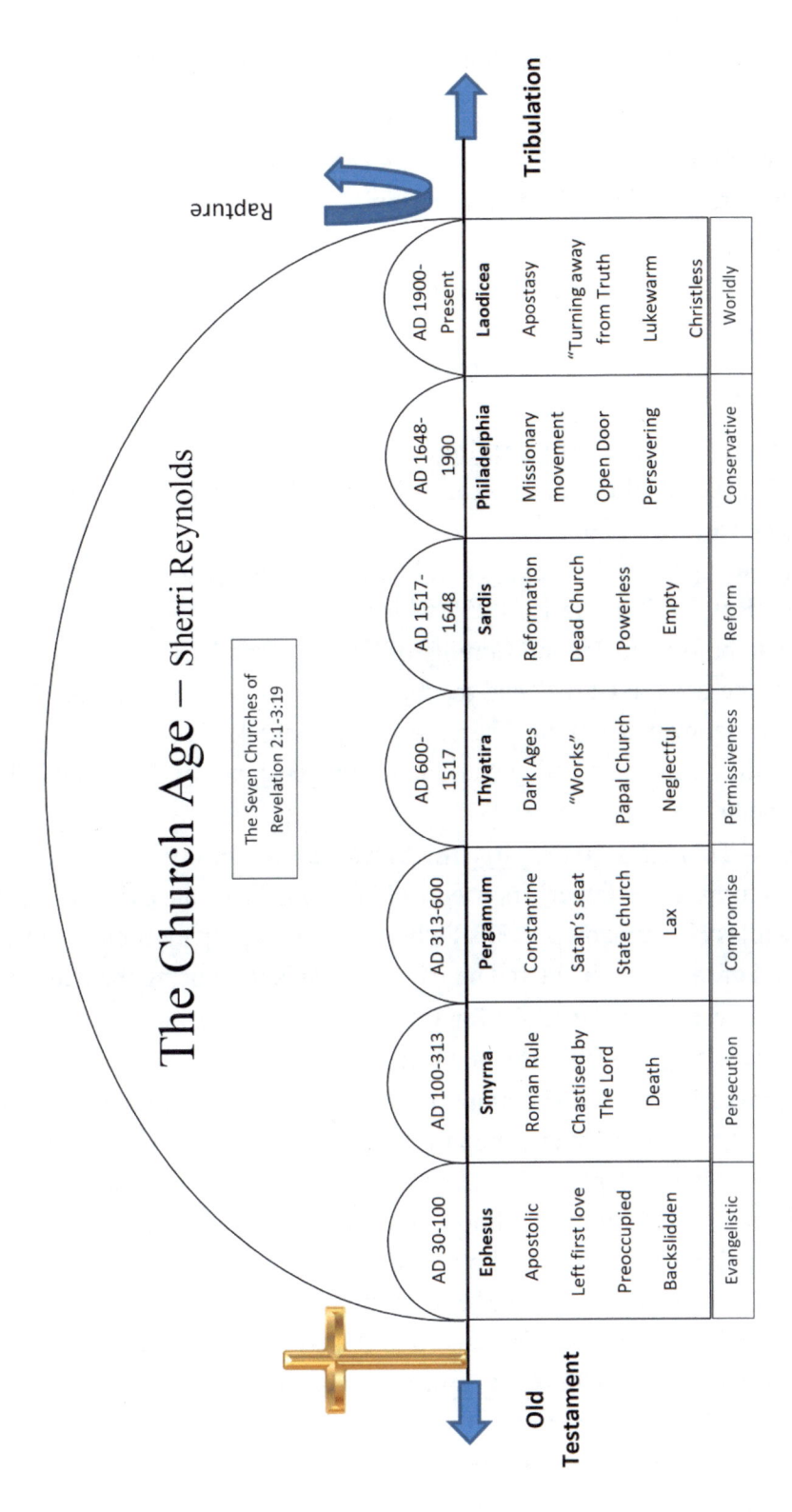

The Church Age – Sherri Reynolds

The Seven Churches of Revelation 2:1-3:19

Old Testament → **Rapture** → **Tribulation**

	Ephesus	Smyrna	Pergamum	Thyatira	Sardis	Philadelphia	Laodicea
	AD 30-100	AD 100-313	AD 313-600	AD 600-1517	AD 1517-1648	AD 1648-1900	AD 1900-Present
	Apostolic	Roman Rule	Constantine	Dark Ages	Reformation	Missionary movement	Apostasy
	Left first love	Chastised by The Lord	Satan's seat	"Works"	Dead Church	Open Door	"Turning away from Truth"
	Preoccupied	Death	State church	Papal Church	Powerless	Persevering	Lukewarm
	Backslidden		Lax	Neglectful	Empty		Christless
	Evangelistic	Persecution	Compromise	Permissiveness	Reform	Conservative	Worldly

Parables in Matt. 13

Sower	Wheat and Tares	Mustard Seed	Leaven	Treasure Hid	Pearl	Dragnet
Verses 3-9	Verses 24-30, 36-43	Verses 31-32	Verses 33-35	Verse 44	Verses 45-46	Verses 47-50

Customs of the Galilean Wedding

1st century wedding customs of the Galilean wedding holds the keys to the return of Christ. His first miracle was at the wedding in Cana.

- **The selection of the bride.**
    - Parents of the groom select a bride for the son.
- **The betrothal – Engagement period.**
    - A one-year contract marked by a ceremony everyone is invited to.
- **At this ceremony, covenants are made.**
    - The bride receives a cup to seal the covenant which she can reject – Matt 26:26-27.
    - If accepted, gifts are exchanged.
- **Also at this ceremony, there is a consecration.**
    - After the bride accepts the cup, the groom does not drink again until the bride comes to the father's house – Matt 26:29.
    - Jesus drank the cup at the Last Supper and will not drink again until the Marriage Supper of the Lamb (Rev 19: 7-9; Mark 14:25), which takes place during the seven-year tribulation and before the Second Coming of Christ – Rev 19:11.
    - The bride is "the dead in Christ" and the raptured saints or "The Church". This will include all the believers from the Church Age – I Thess 4:15-17.
    - "Blessed are they which are called unto the marriage supper of the Lamb" This will include all the OT saints. – Rev 19:9
- **House Preparation – This takes place after the betrothal ceremony.**
    - The groom returns to his father's house to add on rooms. At the ascension of Christ, He told the disciples He was going to His Father's house to prepare rooms – Jn 14:1-3.
    - The bride and groom are considered married but live apart during the betrothal period.
- **The bride needs to be ready day or night for the return of her groom.**
    - She must remain pure as well – II Cor 11:2; Rev 19:8.
- **Only the father knows the day and the hour that he will send his son to go get his bride.**
    - The groom continues to build and prepare a place for his bride until the father approves of the son's new dwelling place. He then tells his son to go get his bride. This is done at midnight based on the Galilean tradition, so the bride must always be prepared.
    - Only the Father knows the day and hour of Christ's return – Matt 24:36.
    - The Father tells the groom to get the bride at midnight – Matt 25:6.
    - Parable of the wise and foolish virgins – Matt 25:1-13.
- **The bride hears the sound of the Shofar (Trumpet) when the groom comes for her.**
    - The trump of God will sound at Christ's return – I Thess 4:16.
- **Wedding guests are given special clothes to wear to the banquet – Matt 22:11.**
    - These garments represent salvation, all those who are saved but are not "The Church": OT saints and tribulation saints.

Seven Annual Jewish Feasts

There are <u>seven</u> annual feasts that God ordained for the Israelites to celebrate each year. These are fulfilled according to Israel, not the church. God's plan is for the redemption of Israel.

1. **Passover – Ex 11:1-12:30; Lev 23:5.**

    - <u>Redemption</u>, the death of Christ /Crucifixion – Matt 27:33-50. Nisan=March/April – AD 33.

2. **Unleavened Bread – Ex 12:8-20; Lev 23:6-8.**

    - <u>Separation</u>/Burial – Matt 27:57-66. Nisan=March/April – AD 33.

3. **First Fruits – Lev 23:9-14.**

    - First <u>produce</u> of a season /Resurrection – Matt 28:1-8. Nisan=March/April – AD 33.

4. **Pentecost – (50 – Jubilee) – Lev 23:15-22.**

    - The <u>Church</u> was born (not fulfilled by the church) – Acts 2:1-4. Sivan=May – AD 33.
    - Presence of the Hoy Spirit rejected by <u>Israel</u> when they taunted the apostles with charges of drunkenness – Acts 2:12-13.

These 4 feasts all take place in the <u>springtime</u> and have all passed. They took place at Christ's first coming. The summer is for planting and growth.

The next 3 feasts take place in the <u>fall</u> and are all future – harvest.

5. **Feast of Trumpets – Lev 23:23-25 – Tishtei=Sept/Oct.**

    - Rosh Hashanah – Also known as "10 Days of <u>Awe</u>" before Yom Kipper.
    - Most people believe this is the <u>Rapture</u> – I Thess 4:16.
    - Shout of the Lord, voice of the archangel, and the <u>trump</u> of God – I Thess 4:16.
    - Some believe this is the <u>Second Coming</u> when Israel is gathered in belief and there is a reconstruction of the Temple before the final battle of Armageddon.

6. **Day of Atonement – Lev 23:26-32 – Tishrei=Sept/Oct.**

    - Yom Kipper – Zech 12:10-14, Rom 11:25-27.
    - Israel's <u>redemption</u> – Deut 4:29-31; Ez 39:28-29.
    - Most believe this is the Second Coming. Those who believe the Feast of Trumpets was the Second Coming believe it is the day Christ enters the <u>East Gate</u> and then the Holy of Holies.
    - There is a new <u>reaction</u> of Israel to the Redeemer's Death. There is a believing Jewish remnant at the end of the Tribulation before Gentile armies attack Jerusalem. All of the house of Israel is saved in a day – Ez 39:21-22.

7. **Feast of Tabernacle – Lev 23:33-44 – Tishrei=Sept/Oct.**

    - <u>Millennial</u> kingdom reign – Rev 20:1-7.

Seven Annual Feasts of Israel – Sherri Reynolds

Gregorian Calendar – January is the first month of the year

January	February	March	April	May	June	July	August	Sept	October	Nov	Dec
1	2	3	4	5	6	7	8	9	10	11	12

Jewish Calendar – Nisan is the first month of the year

Shevat	Adar	Nisan	Iyar	Sivan	Tammuz	Av	Elul	Tishrei	Cheshvan	Kislev	Tevet
11	12	1	2	3	4	5	6	7	8	9	10

Passover	Unleavened Bread	First fruits	Feast of Weeks	Feast of Trumpets	Day of Atonement	Feast of Tabernacles
Death of Christ	Burial of Christ	Resurrection of Christ	Pentecost	Rapture	Israel's Repentance	The Millennium
AD 33	AD 33	AD 33	AD 33	Beginning of Tribulation	After Second Coming	After Israel's Repentance

CHAPTER 5

The Rapture

Rapture

John 14:1-3

- I go to prepare a <u>place</u> for you.
- If I go, I will <u>come again</u> and receive you unto Myself.
- He will <u>descend</u> from His Father's house – I Thess 4:16.

Signs that the Second Coming (not the Rapture) is near.

- Rebirth of <u>Israel</u> as a nation, May 14, 1948. They are back in the land – Is 66:8; Ez 36:24.
- The Middle East is in <u>crisis</u> – Matt 24:6-7.
- Crisis over <u>oil</u> – Ez 38:12-13.
- Reformation of a united <u>Europe</u> (EU) already exists – Dan 2:41-43.
- Global economy is already a <u>reality</u> – Rev 6:5-6.
- Growth of militant radical <u>Islam</u> – Ez 38-39.
- <u>Weapons</u> of mass destruction have already been invented – Rev 6:7-8.
- Spread of <u>evil</u> – Luke 17:26-30.
- Apostasy – I Tim 4:1-5; II Tim 3:1-5, 4:1-4.
- The Holy Spirit restrains evil right now through the <u>church</u> – II Thess 2:7.
- There will be a strong <u>delusion</u> after the rapture, a distorted Gospel – II Thess 2:11.
- If Christmas decorations are up in the stores, that tells us that Thanksgiving is even sooner. If we are already seeing signs of the Second Coming, that tells us that the <u>Rapture</u> is even sooner.

From the Cross to Eternity

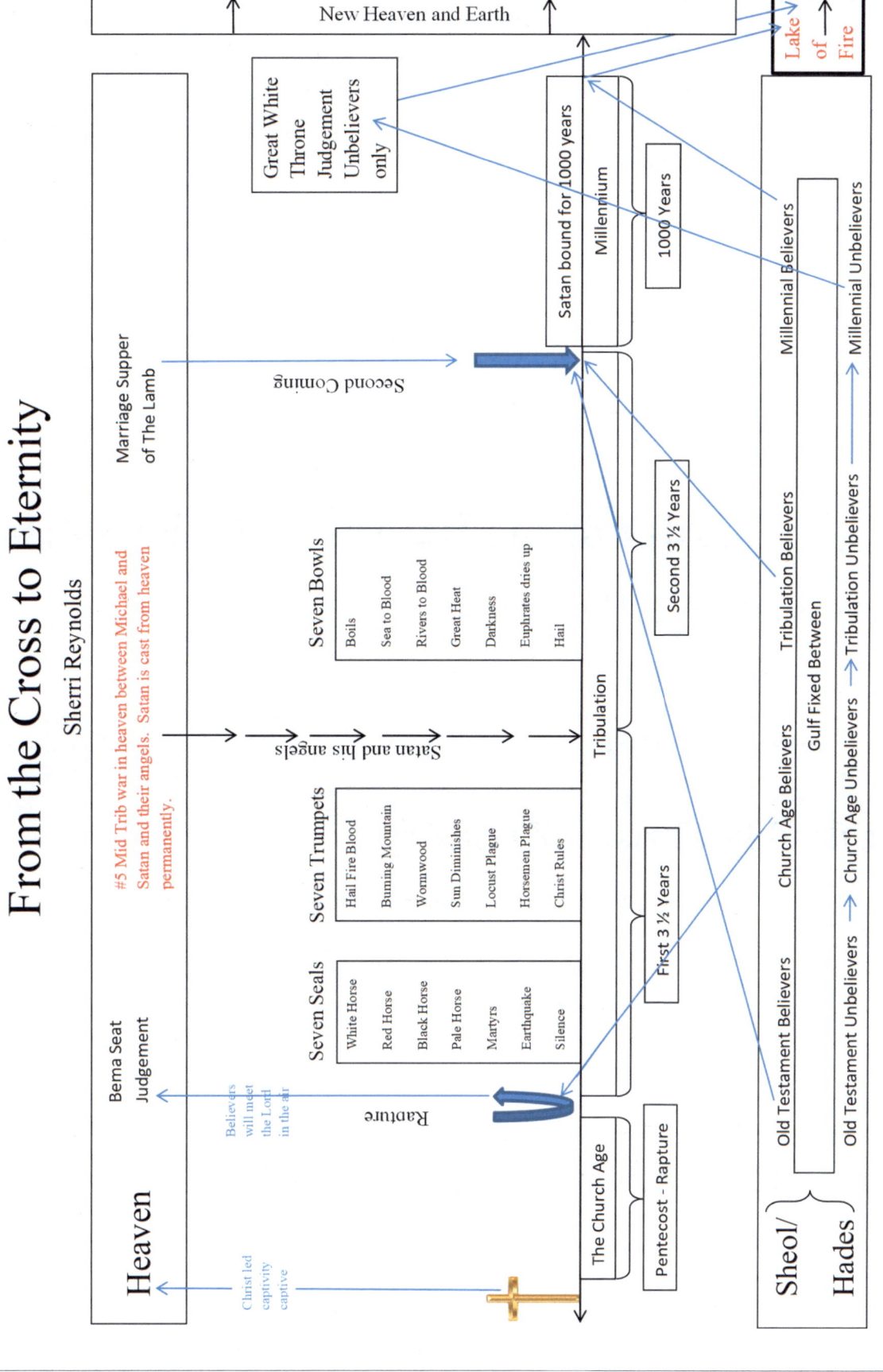

Sherri Reynolds

Heaven

- Bema Seat Judgement
- Marriage Supper of The Lamb
- #5 Mid Trib war in heaven between Michael and Satan and their angels. Satan is cast from heaven permanently.
- Great White Throne Judgement Unbelievers only
- New Heaven and Earth
- Satan bound for 1000 years / Millennium / 1000 Years

Christ led captivity captive

Believers will meet the Lord in the air

Rapture → **Second Coming**

Satan and his angels →

Seven Seals
- White Horse
- Red Horse
- Black Horse
- Pale Horse
- Martyrs
- Earthquake
- Silence

Seven Trumpets
- Hail Fire Blood
- Burning Mountain
- Wormwood
- Sun Diminishes
- Locust Plague
- Horsemen Plague
- Christ Rules

Seven Bowls
- Boils
- Sea to Blood
- Rivers to Blood
- Great Heat
- Darkness
- Euphrates dries up
- Hail

The Church Age | Pentecost - Rapture | First 3 ½ Years | Tribulation | Second 3 ½ Years

Sheol / Hades
- Old Testament Believers → Church Age Believers → Tribulation Believers → Millennial Believers
- Gulf Fixed Between
- Old Testament Unbelievers → Church Age Unbelievers → Tribulation Unbelievers → Millennial Unbelievers

Lake of Fire

I Thess 4:13-18

- The word Rapture does <u>not</u> appear in the Bible.
  - The English words used in I Thess 4:17 are "caught up", which was translated from the original Greek words "snatched out <u>speedily</u>", taken out of harms way speedily.
  - The word Rapture is the <u>Latin</u> translation of the words "rapio" or "rapturo" (Hindson, 2014).
- <u>No</u> Biblical, prophetic event needs to take place before the Rapture occurs.
  - It is the <u>next</u> event on God's prophetic timeline.
- It will only be <u>witnessed</u> by believers.
  - No one else will <u>see</u> Christ.
- Christ will not <u>touch</u> down to the earth.
  - We will meet Him in the <u>clouds</u> – I Thess 4:17.

Order of the Rapture – I Thess 4:14-18

Three Sounds- I Thess 4:16.

- The Lord will <u>shout</u>.
- The <u>voice</u> of the archangel.
- The <u>trump</u> of God.

The dead in Christ will rise first.

- Corruptible ashes are made incorruptible <u>bodies</u> and reunited with their spirits – I Thess 4:16.
- This will only be the NT believers, the Church, the <u>Bride</u> of Christ.
- The OT saints will be resurrected <u>after</u> Armageddon but before the Millennium – Dan 12:2, 13.

We who are alive in Christ will rise and reunite with the resurrected believers and Christ in the air.

- We are all given a <u>new</u> immortal body – I Cor 15:51-53.
- Then both will be caught up together in the clouds to meet the Lord in the <u>air</u> and return to The Father's House with Jesus – I Thess 4:17.

All of this will happen in the twinkling of an eye – I Cor 15:52.

From then on, we will always be with the Lord – I Thess 4:17.

The NT Church will be removed from the earth at this time.

- The Church is the <u>agent</u> through which the Holy Spirit currently works.
- He <u>indwells</u> the believer – Rom 8:9-11.
- Since the Church is gone, the Holy Spirit will continue to minister during the Tribulation as He did in the <u>OT</u>, when He came upon people and sometimes left (I Sam 16:14), but the influence of worldwide believers will not exist.
- <u>Evil</u> will have full reign.

NOTES:

CHAPTER 6

The Tribulation

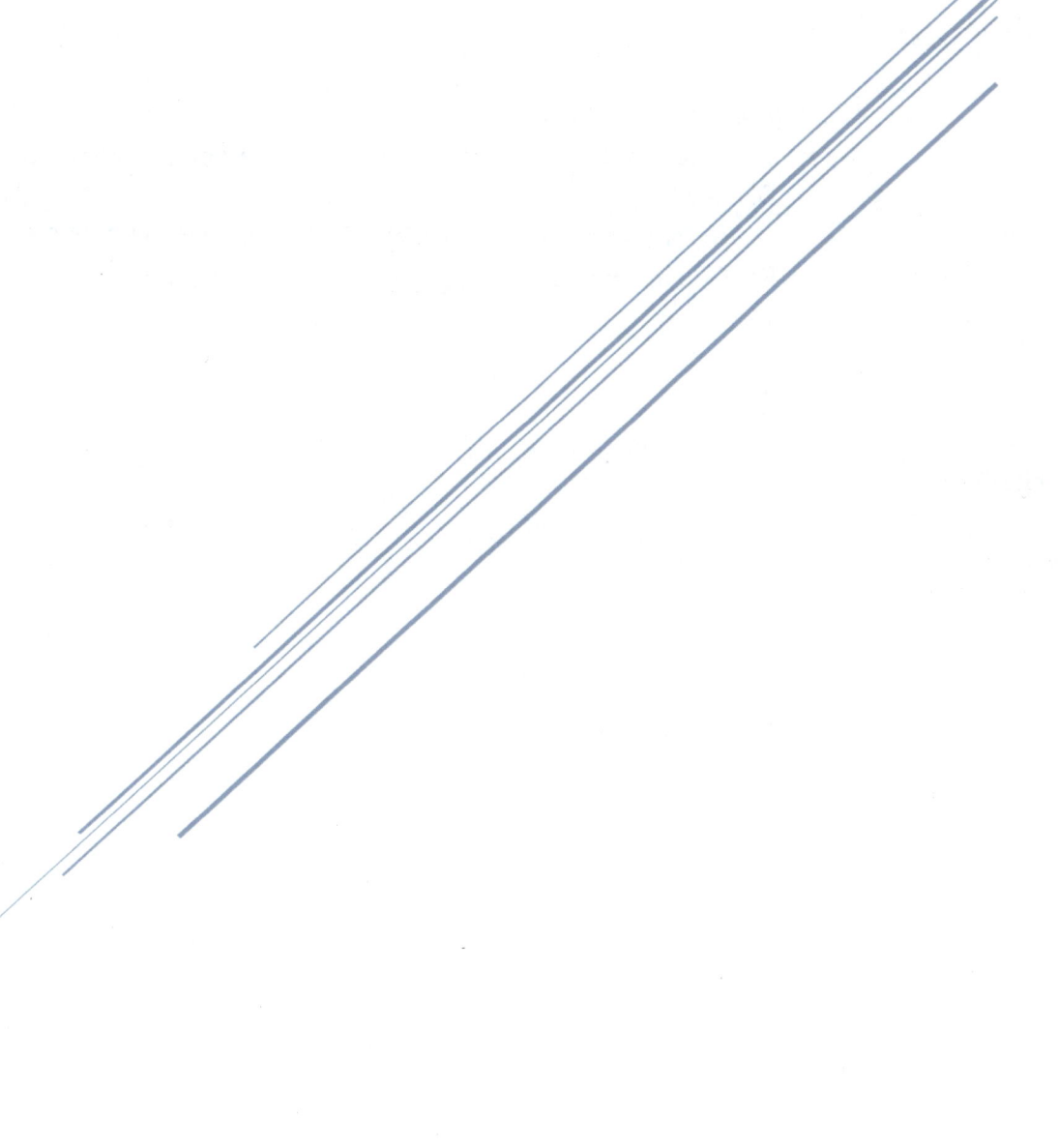

Tribulation Defined

- The definition of Tribulation is a cause of great <u>trouble</u> or suffering.
- According to the Bible, The Tribulation is a seven-year period <u>after</u> the Church (saved) have been raptured to heaven and before the Second Coming of Christ takes place – Rev 11:2-3; 12:6,7,14; 13:5.
- During this time, God's attention <u>returns</u> to His people, the children of Israel – Dan 9:24-27.
- What takes place is a combination of God's wrath (Rev 6:17), Satan's fury (Rev 12:12), and the evil nature of <u>man</u> run wild. It will be as in the days of Noah – Gen 6:5.

Tribulation Purpose

- The <u>purpose</u> of the Tribulation is two-fold:
    - To bring <u>conversion</u> to the nation of Israel and prepare them for her Messiah – Dan 9:24.
        - The Tribulation is <u>Daniel's</u> 70th week – Daniel 9:24-27.
    - For God to pour out His <u>judgement</u> on the unbelieving nations of the world – Rev 16:1.

NOTES:

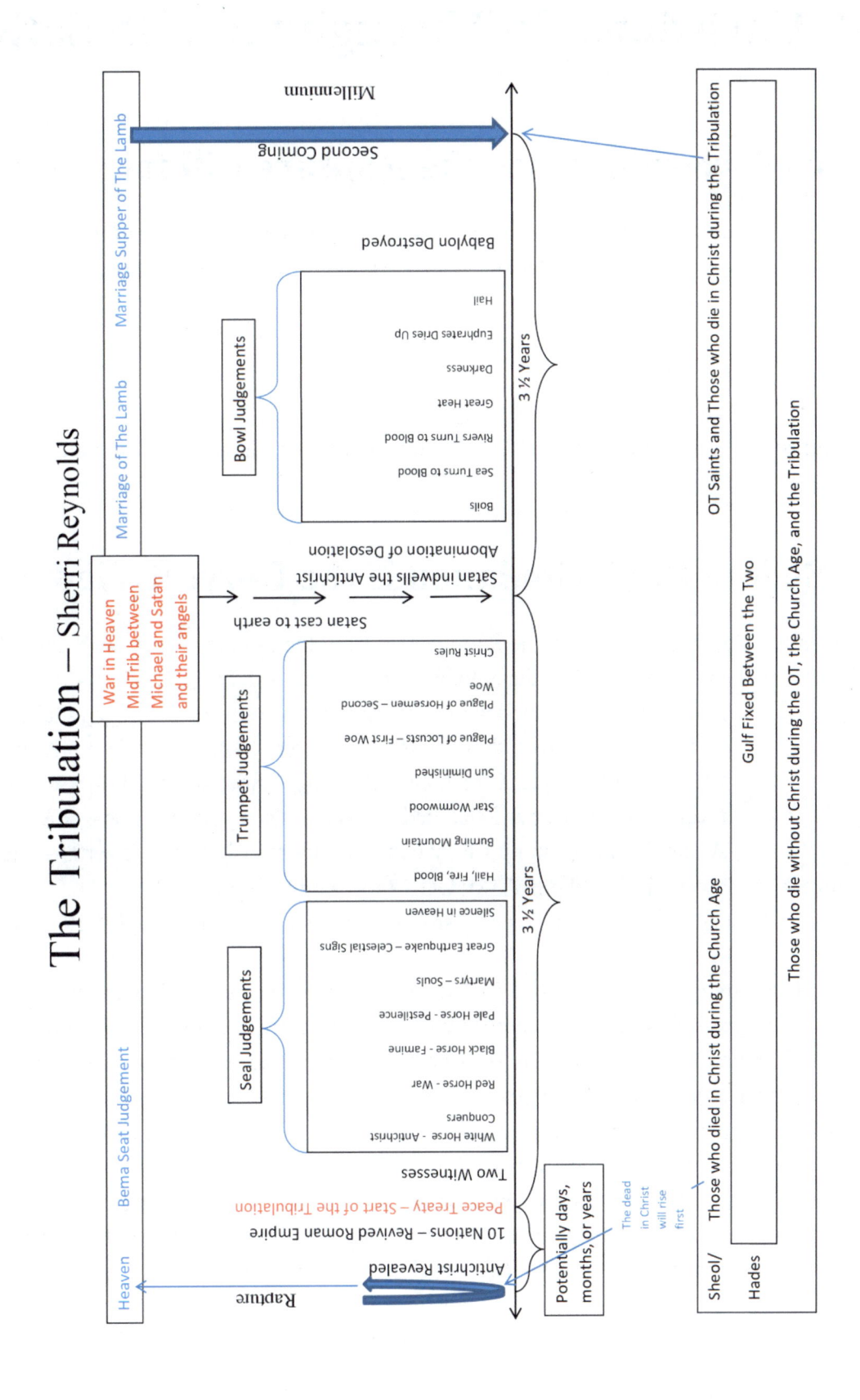

The Tribulation – Sherri Reynolds

Heaven timeline (left column, top to bottom): Bema Seat Judgement → Marriage of The Lamb → Marriage Supper of The Lamb

Mid-Tribulation event (red): War in Heaven — MidTrib between Michael and Satan and their angels

Earth timeline (bottom to top):

- Rapture
- Antichrist Revealed
- 10 Nations – Revived Roman Empire
- Peace Treaty – Start of the Tribulation *(red)*
- Potentially days, months, or years *(before Tribulation)*
- Two Witnesses
- The dead in Christ will rise first

First 3 ½ Years — Seal Judgements:
- White Horse – Antichrist Conquers
- Red Horse – War
- Black Horse – Famine
- Pale Horse – Pestilence
- Martyrs – Souls
- Great Earthquake – Celestial Signs
- Silence in Heaven

Trumpet Judgements:
- Hail, Fire, Blood
- Burning Mountain
- Star Wormwood
- Sun Diminished
- Plague of Locusts – First Woe
- Plague of Horsemen – Second Woe
- Christ Rules

Mid-Tribulation transitions:
- Satan cast to earth
- Satan indwells the Antichrist
- Abomination of Desolation

Second 3 ½ Years — Bowl Judgements:
- Boils
- Sea Turns to Blood
- Rivers Turns to Blood
- Great Heat
- Darkness
- Euphrates Dries Up
- Hail

- Babylon Destroyed
- Second Coming
- Millennium

Afterlife (bottom box — Sheol / Hades):

OT Saints and Those who die in Christ during the Tribulation	Those who died in Christ during the Church Age
Gulf Fixed Between the Two	
Those who die without Christ during the OT, the Church Age, and the Tribulation	

Will Christians Go Through the Tribulation?

There are 5 views of when the Rapture will take place:

- **Pre-Tribulation** – Christ comes to rapture the Church <u>before</u> the wrath of God.
- **Partial Rapture** – Only <u>faithful</u> believers are raptured pre-tribulation. Carnal believers are raptured later.
- **Mid-Tribulation** – Christ raptures believers <u>3 ½</u> years into the Tribulation and are raptured with the two witness – Rev 11:12.
- **Post-Tribulation** – Rapture takes place <u>after</u> the Tribulation.
- **No Rapture** – Believers <u>endure</u> the Tribulation and move right into the Millennium.

Why I Believe Pre-Tribulation is the Correct View

- Paul teaches that in the last days, the falling away from the faith (apostasy) will come <u>first</u>, followed by the rapture, and then the antichrist is revealed – II Thess 2:1-3.
    - Some first century believers thought that the Rapture had <u>already</u> taken place. They were concerned they missed it and were living in the Tribulation.
    - Paul taught them that Christians will go <u>up</u>. Christ comes FOR believers, and we meet Him in the air and that had not taken place yet – I Thess 4:17.
    - At the Second Coming Christ comes all the way back to the earth – Zech 14:4.
- Believers are delivered <u>FROM</u> not THROUGH the wrath to come.
    - It is a specific <u>wrath</u> that He promises to deliver us from – I Thess 1:9-10, I Thess 5:9, Rev 3:10.
    - If we are currently still in the Philadelphia church age and overlapping the Laodicea church age, God promises that He will "Keep us <u>from</u> the hour of temptation" (Tribulation). He will rapture the true believers and leave the apostate church (unbelievers) to go through the Tribulation – Rev 3:7-11.
- The Church is not mentioned as being on the earth during the seven-year tribulation – Rev 6-18.
    - The <u>last</u> mention of the church is Rev 3:22.
    - The word "church" appears <u>seven</u> times between Rev 1 and the end of Rev 3.
    - In Rev 4:1, John is taken up to heaven ("come up hither") for the rest of the book of Revelation, which is <u>symbolic</u> of the church being raptured.
    - The <u>Bridegroom</u> has come and the Bride of Christ is in heaven.
    - The Marriage Supper of the Lamb takes place in heaven <u>while</u> the Tribulation is happening on earth – Rev 19:7-10.

- The Second Coming of Christ takes place <u>after</u> that – Rev 19:11-16.
  - Some believe that the Rapture takes place at the end of the Tribulation and we as believers will go <u>through</u> the Tribulation.
  - If the Church is raptured at the end of the Tribulation, there will be no physical body humans to <u>repopulate</u> the earth during the Millennium. Also, if there is a Rapture at the end of the Tribulation, there would be no need for a separation of the sheep and goats before the Millennium – Matt 25:32-46.
    - "sheep" – physical bodied <u>believers</u> who enter into the Millennium.
    - "goats" – physical bodied <u>unbelievers</u> who are sent to hell.
    - "brethren" – physical bodied <u>Jews</u> who enter into the Millennium.
  - All <u>unsaved</u> are sent directly to hell at this time and all saved humans, along with the glorified body believers who have returned with Christ from heaven at His second coming, move directly into the Millennium – Matt 25:46, Rev 20:7-10.
- Jesus is talking to His disciples about the end times and leaves the final generation a stern warning – "watch …pray…that ye may be accounted <u>worthy</u> to ESCAPE all things that shall come to pass" – Luke 21:34-36.
  - We are told to look for <u>Christ</u>, not the antichrist – Phil 3:20, Heb 9:28.
  - The Bridegroom's return is imminent (Matt 25:1-13), but not even God the <u>Son</u> knows the day or hour – Matt 24:36.
  - If we go through part or all of the Tribulation, we have been given a very <u>specific</u> timeline (7 years, with specific events happening at specific times).
- If the resurrection of the saints, the rapture of those saints, and the church did not occur pre-tribulation and we were to go through the Tribulation to endure the wrath of God, where is the "<u>comfort</u>" Paul is talking about? – I Thess 4:18.
- If the Rapture is post-tribulation, we would <u>rush</u> to heaven, have no time for the Bema Seat Judgement, Marriage of the Lamb, and the Marriage Supper of the Lamb, and immediately return to earth with Christ for His Second Coming.
  - What is the purpose in that? Personally, I do not want to rush through my supper. No <u>bride</u> wants to hurry through her wedding reception. The Groom has waited over 6,000 years to be reunited with His bride. I do not think He wants to rush through it either.

CHAPTER 7

What Happens in Heaven During the Tribulation

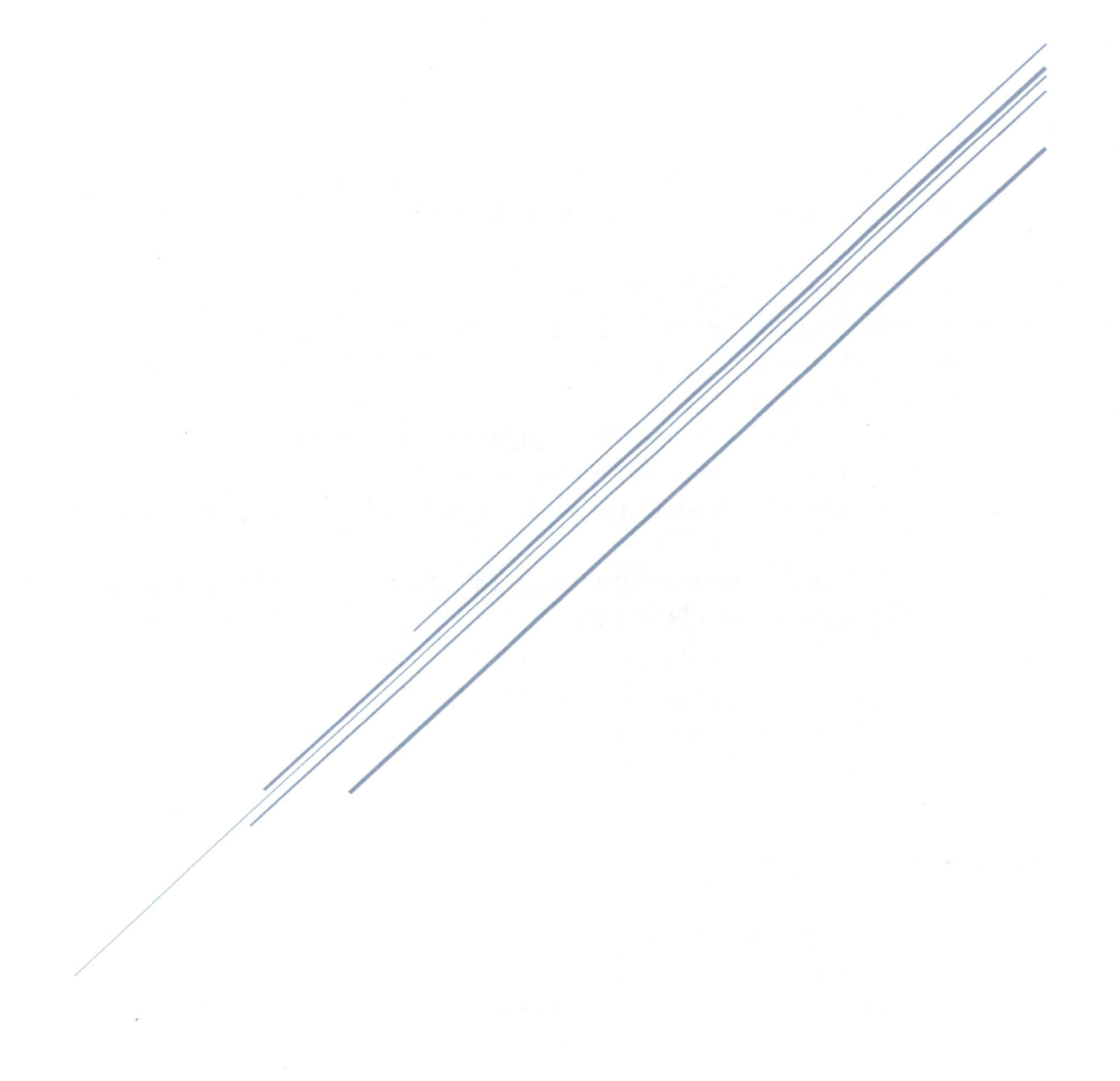

What Happens in Heaven During the Tribulation?

God reveals that believers will all be judged – Ps 62:12; Matt 5:11-12, 16:27; Rom 14:10-12; II Cor 5:10, Rev 22:12.

Bema Seat Judgement – Greek for "Judgement Seat"

- Our Lord Jesus Christ Himself is the judge – II Tim 4:8.
  - He will judge the works of the redeemed on an individual basis to determine the degree of rewards to be given – I Cor 3:13, Rev 11:18.
- All who stand here are saved.
  - Their eternal destiny in heaven is secure – Eph 1:13, 4:30.
  - We will be judged at this point for everything we have done whether good or bad, not for our salvation.
  - We would not be at this judgement if we were not saved.
- Works will be judged to determine motive and character – II Cor 5:10.
- All of your life, good and bad, will pass through the Refiner's fire – I Cor 3:12-15.
  - The bad is burned off.
  - The good remains. You will be rewarded for works done in the power and for the glory of God – Gold, silver, and precious stone.
  - All other works are burnt up – wood, hay, and stubble – and you will suffer loss from them.
  - All of these works done in the flesh and all of your sins, as a believer, are covered by the blood of Christ – I Cor 3:15.
- We all will stand before the judgement seat of Christ – Rom 14:10.
- Lay up for yourselves treasures in heaven – Matt 6:19-21.
  - You have the opportunity now to make a difference for your eternity. Do not let it pass by.

Crowns to be Earned

- **The Incorruptible Crown – "Victor's Crown".**
  - For the one who strives for the mastery, is temperate in all things, and submission of the body (lust of the flesh), purged from the pleasures of this world in order to be of profitable service for the Lord – I Cor 9:25-27.

- **The Crown of Rejoicing – "Soul winner's crown".**
    - For those who lead <u>souls</u> to Christ – I Thess 2:19-20.
- **The Crown of Life – "Martyr's crown"/"Sufferer's crown".**
    - For the one who endured temptation not <u>yielding</u> – James 1:12, suffered much through the trials of this life with a sweet Christian spirit – Matt 5:12, Luke 6:23. Also, for those who have been faithful unto death – Rev 2:10.
- **The Crown of Glory – "Shepherd's crown"/"Pastor's crown".**
    - For those who <u>feed</u> the flock, teach the Word of God, and help other Christians mature – I Pet 5:1-4.
- **The Crown of Righteousness.**
    - For those who anticipate with <u>great</u> eagerness the appearing of Jesus Christ and live a righteous, holy life. – II Tim 4:8.

Good Works with Good Motives

- **Witness** – Matt 5:16.
    - One who lets their light shine, <u>represents</u> Christ, and lives a pure life.
- **Worship** – Matt 26:7-10.
    - Good deeds are a form of <u>worship</u> to God – Matt 6:4.
    - Do good deeds in secret and God will reward you <u>openly</u>.
- **Generosity** – I Tim 6:18.
    - Giving with a proper <u>motive</u>.
- **Keeping of God's law** – Ps 19:9-11.
    - There is <u>great</u> reward.
- **Compassion** – Matt 10:42.
    - Even a cup of cold water in His <u>name</u> has its reward.
- **Love your enemies, do good, lend, hoping for nothing in return** – Luke 6:35.
    - Your reward shall be <u>great.</u>
- **Your labor in the Lord** – I Cor 15:58.
    - Is not in <u>vain</u> in the Lord.
- **Your confidence in God** – Heb 10:35.
    - Brings <u>great</u> reward – Rev 3:11.

Good Works with Wrong Motives

- **To impress men** – Matt 6:1-6, 16-18; Gal 5:26.
- **Selfishness and laziness**.
  - We are robbed and there will be loss – Matt 10:42, I Cor 3:15, 9:17-18.
- **Enticed away from serving the Lord** – Rev 3:11.
  - You can lose your rewards and what you have accomplished for Christ – II John v.8.
  - You will not lose your salvation, but you will lose your reward – I Cor 3:15.

Attitude of a Christian Toward this Judgement

- **Judgement will be a time of rejoicing and should not be looked at as a time of fear** – Jude v.24.
  - Your sins will not be plastered across some heavenly screen for all to see.
- **The greatest rewards are those that God gives.**
- **Your faithfulness on earth will be directly related to your stature in heaven and your place or rank during the Millennium, Christ's earthly reign.**
  - II Tim 2:12; Rev 5:10, 20:6, and in the eternal state – Rev 22:5.
- **God told Abraham that "I AM" was his shield and his exceeding great reward**.
  - Gen 15:1.

Results of the Bema Seat

- We will cast the crowns that we have earned at the feet of Jesus in thanksgiving for what He has done – Rev 4:10-11.
  - We should be ambitious to receive as many crowns as possible.
- We will receive clothing signifying the kinds of works we have done which are the wedding garments we will wear at the wedding ceremony (Marriage of the Lamb).
  - Rev 7:9, 19:8.
- We will be assigned places of authority in the coming Millennium and eternal state based upon our faithfulness to God, as well as the influence we left behind, when we were on earth.
  - Matt 19:27-28; Luke 19:12-27; I Cor 6:1-2; Rev 20:4, 21:24, 22:5.

After the Bema Seat

- The Bride of Christ makes herself <u>ready</u> for the Marriage of The Lamb.
  - Rom 14:10, I Cor 3:10-15, II Cor 5:10, Rev 19:7-8.

War in Heaven at the Midpoint of the Tribulation

- This is a <u>war</u> between Michael the Archangel with his army and Satan with his army.
- Satan and his angels are <u>permanently</u> banned from Heaven, never to return again – Rev 12:7-13.

Marriage of The Lamb – Rev 19:7-8

Marriage Supper of The Lamb – Rev 19:9

- This takes place at the <u>end</u> of the Tribulation.
  - Matt 8:11, Mark 14:25, Luke 13:29, 14:12-15.

NOTES:

CHAPTER 8

What Happens on Earth – First 3 ½ Years

What Will Happen on Earth During the Tribulation?

Immediately after the Rapture

- **The <u>Church</u> is removed from the earth, not the Holy Spirit – I Thess 4:16-17, II Thess 2:6-7.**
    - The Church is the Holy Spirit's agent to <u>restrain</u>. There will be no more influence from the Spirit of God through the Church and therefore, unrestrained evil will dominate.
    - The Holy Spirit does continue to <u>minister</u> during the Tribulation as He did in the OT when He came upon people (I Sam 16:13) and, in some cases, left someone – I Sam 16:14.
    - He will seal and <u>protect</u> the two witnesses, Moses and Elijah, and the 144,000 (Rev:7:3-4, 11:1-6), and also aid Tribulation believers to live holy lives – Rev 20:4.
- **Will those who have heard the Gospel before the Rapture be able to get saved <u>after</u> the Rapture?**
    - If they can at all, it will be extremely difficult because of the "strong <u>delusion</u>" that God will send on them – II Thess 2:10-11.
- **The antichrist is <u>revealed</u> – Rev 6:1-2, II Thess 2:3-6.**
    - He will present himself as a man of <u>peace</u> on a white horse, which indicates peace, and with a bow but not an arrow (Rev 6:2), but in reality, he is Satan's agent rising from the abyss (Bottomless Pit – Rev 11:7) most likely a demonic spirit in a human body.
    - He will rise out of the <u>10</u> nations revived Roman Empire pictured as the ten toes in Danial 2.

- **The first <u>battle</u> of Gog and Magog – Ez 38-39.**
    - This battle could <u>potentially</u> happen at this point.
    - Some place this war anywhere shortly before the Rapture to shortly after the peace treaty is <u>confirmed</u> by the antichrist.
    - Some believe this war is what paves the way for the antichrist to confirm the peace treaty with Israel which <u>starts</u> the seven-year tribulation time clock ticking.

- I believe this war takes place <u>after</u> the peace treaty is signed because Ez 38:11 says, "They will go up to the land of unwalled villages to those who are at rest, and dwell safely". This would indicate that the peace treaty has already been signed. A coalition of nations will rise up against Israel. This coalition of nations is led by Russia.

Battle of Gog and Magog – List of nations in Ez. 38 and 39.

- **Gog** – <u>Title</u> of a ruler.
- **Magog** – former <u>Soviet Union</u> nations, area north of the Caspian and Black seas – Russia, Ukraine, Kazakhstan, Kyrgyzstan, Uzbekistan, Turkmenistan, Tajikistan, Azerbaijan, Georgia, and possibly parts of Afghanistan.
- **Rosh** – "most distinctly north", "far north" – <u>Russia</u>.
- **Cush** – Ethiopia, Somalia, and Sudan.
- **Put** – Libya.
- **Mesheck and Tubal**, (Some think these are the <u>cities</u> of Moscow (in Russia) and Tobolsk, or Mushki and Tobolsk which are both in Turkey) – present day nation of Turkey.
- **Gomer** – <u>Germany</u>, Austria, Poland, and part of Turkey, or land of the Galatians in Greece.
- **Togarmah – Phrygia** – western kingdom in <u>Asia Minor</u>, part of Turkey.
- **Persia – Iran**, Afghanistan, Pakistan.
- **Iran**.
- **The king of the north** – <u>Syria</u>.
- **The king of the south** – <u>Egypt</u>.
- **All of these nations are <u>Islamic</u> except Russia** and will be in a coalition against Israel. Russia will finance it and wants the spoils – Ez 38:12.
  - Persia is the <u>bed</u> of militant Islam and anti-Semitic hatred.
  - It is the <u>prime</u> player in human trafficking, key trans-shipment point of heroin into Europe, state sponsor of terrorism, has uranium enrichment capacities, and hates Israel.
  - Iran desires to <u>eliminate</u> Israel, says it must be wiped off the map, and anyone who recognizes Israel will burn in the fire of Islamic nation's fury.
- **Nations that will <u>not</u> invade Israel**, even protest the invasion – Ez 28:13.
  - Sheba and Dedan, Saudi Arabia (Arabian Peninsula nations including Oman, Kuwait, and United Arab Emirates), the merchants of Tarshish (Western Europe, Spain), and their <u>young lions</u> (potentially Canada, Australia, New Zealand, African colonies, and what is left of the USA).

- o These nations <u>object</u> but will not or are unable to help.
- **There is no possible <u>human</u> defense for Israel**.
  - o They know it and the rest of the world knows it. The only thing that will save Israel is <u>intervention</u> from God – Ez 38:22-23.
- **Purpose of the invasion**.
  - o Seize the land, <u>steal</u> the wealth, and wholesale slaughter of Israel's people – Ex 38:12-13.
  - o Massive <u>oil</u> fields were found in Israel in the late 1990's.
  - o Currently Israel has over 7,200 millionaires some due to the <u>high-tech</u> revolution (Jeramiah, 2008).
  - o There is an estimated $1 trillion worth of salt, bromine, potash, and magnesium chloride in the <u>Dead Sea</u> alone.
  - o In 2019, large <u>oil</u> deposits were found off the cost of Israel in the Mediterranean Sea.
  - o Russia was humiliated in the war between <u>Syria</u> and Israel in 1982. Over 80 Russian built planes were blown out of the sky, retaliation.
- **Invasion Tactic**.
  - o Attack from the <u>north</u>. Russia will be the leader. They will assemble on the mountains of Israel on northern border with Syria, Lebanon, and Jordan – Ez 38:8.
- **Conclusion of this war, Intervention of God – Ez 38:18-39:7.**
  - o <u>God</u> miraculously delivers Israel.
  - o There is a massive <u>convulsion</u> of the earth – Ez 38:19-20.
  - o Confusion and panic cause attacking troops to begin killing one another – Ez 38:21.
  - o There will be disease and calamities from the <u>sky</u> including torrential rain, hailstorms, fire, and burning sulfur – Ez 38:22.
- **Aftermath of God's victory – Israel turns to God.**
  - o There is a nationwide <u>spiritual</u> awakening, revival and return to God – Ez 39:22.
  - o God is the One Who defeats all these nations, but the antichrist will <u>usurp</u> the victory – Dan 9:27.
- **It takes 7 months to bury the dead and 7 years to burn all the weapons – Ez 39:9-14.**
  - o The <u>Israelites</u> are the ones burning the weapons and they flee Israel shortly after mid-tribulation – Ez 39:9, Matt 24:15-20.
- **There will be a brief time period between the Rapture and the Tribulation, <u>before</u> the seven-year time clock begins.**
  - o It <u>could</u> be a matter of days, months, or a few years.
  - o When the peace treaties, allowing for sacrifices in the Temple, are <u>confirmed</u> (they are already established) between the antichrist and Israel, the seven-year Tribulation clock actually begins to tick – Dan 9:27.
  - o This <u>gap</u> could also account for the 7 years that Israel will be burning the weapons from the first Gog and Magog war (Ez 39:9-10). Israel will flee to the wilderness at the mid-point of the tribulation (Rev 12:6) so they will have stopped burning at that point.

First 3 ½ Years of Tribulation

- **As a result of Israel's resounding victory of the first Gog and Magog war** (Ez 38:18-23), Israel is respected as a major world power, new <u>alliances</u> will form led by the antichrist (10 nation confederacy – EU).
- **The Temple in Jerusalem is rebuilt, sacrifices <u>resume</u>, and Israel will live in safety – Dan 9:27.**
  - In order for sacrifices to cease halfway through the Tribulation, the Temple will have had to be <u>rebuilt</u> and daily sacrifices installed again.
- **China and North Korea will <u>conquer</u> surrounding lands.**
  - They will make a pact with <u>Japan</u> and begin their march east as the Tribulation progresses – Rev 16:12.
- **God will still expend incredible effort to <u>save</u> man.**
  - Two witnesses will preach for 3 ½ years (Rev 11:3), 144,000 witnesses will spread the Gospel (Rev 7:3-8), an <u>angel</u> will proclaim the Gospel (Rev 14:6), and natural disasters will occur (Rev 11:13) to turn men to God.
- **Two Witnesses**
  - Shortly after the treaties are confirmed, two witnesses begin to preach salvation for 3 ½ years. They preach from <u>Temple Mount</u>. They have unbelievable power over death, drought, and disease, have the ability to prophecy, call down fire from heaven, and are protected by God. Many Jews are saved – Rev 11:3-6.
  - One of these witnesses is <u>Elijah</u> – Mal 4:5.
    - There are theories that the other witness is <u>Enoch</u> because neither of these men died while on earth. They were both individually raptured, but there is no scriptural backing for Enoch being the second witness – Gen 5:24, II Kings 2:11.
    - The other theory is that the men are Elijah (power to shut heaven so that it did not rain – I Kings 17:1, James 5:17) and <u>Moses</u> (turned water into blood – Ex 7:14-25) – Rev 11:6.
    - Scripture specifically says that Elijah will be sent back <u>before</u> the Day of the Lord (Mal 4:5). Also, Moses and Elijah appeared with Christ on the Mount of Transfiguration – Matt 17:1-3.
    - These two witnesses are likened to the two <u>olive trees</u> in Zech 4:1-14. As a result, there are 144,000 sealed and protected male Jewish witnesses (12,000 from each tribe of Israel) that evangelize bringing a great harvest of souls - Rev 7:3-8.

- **There are a <u>series</u> of 7 Seal Judgements (Rev 6:1-8:1), 7 Trumpet Judgements (Rev 8:2-9:21, 11:15-19), and 7 Bowl Judgements (Rev 15:1-16:21) which will span the whole 7-year Tribulation period.**
    - Some of the charts lay them out in exact chronological order. There is a possibility that they <u>overlap</u> with each other greatly.

- **There is a 7 sealed scroll judgement in heaven which is the title deed to the earth (Rev 5:1).**
    - The "book" is a <u>scroll</u> sealed with seven seals.
    - It belonged to God the <u>Son</u> when He created the earth – John 1:1-3, Col 1:15-19, Heb 1:2.
    - Authority of it was given <u>temporarily</u> to Satan at the Fall of man. Satan tempted to give it back to Jesus in the wilderness after Jesus was baptized if Jesus would worship him – Matt 4:8-10.
    - Even <u>nature</u> itself groans from Satan's temporary rule – Rom 8:22.
    - John wept in heaven because he thought no one was worthy to open the seals – Rev 5:4.
    - There is only One Who is <u>worthy</u>, The Lion of the tribe of Judah, the Root of David (Rev 5:5), The Lamb of God (Rev 5:6), because He was slain and redeemed us to God by His blood – Rev 5:9.

- **Christ releases each of these 7 judgements on the earth as part of the beginning process of <u>purifying</u> it before He is able to take it back and reign over it and have dominion over it.**
    - According to some charts, all 7 of these judgements take place in the <u>first</u> 3 ½ years of the tribulation.
    - Others have them <u>spread</u> over the 7 years.
    - The two witnesses and an additional 144,000 Jewish male servants of God who are sealed in their foreheads who preach salvation during this time are protected against the <u>wrath</u> of God – Rev 7:3-4, Rev 11:1-6.

NOTES:

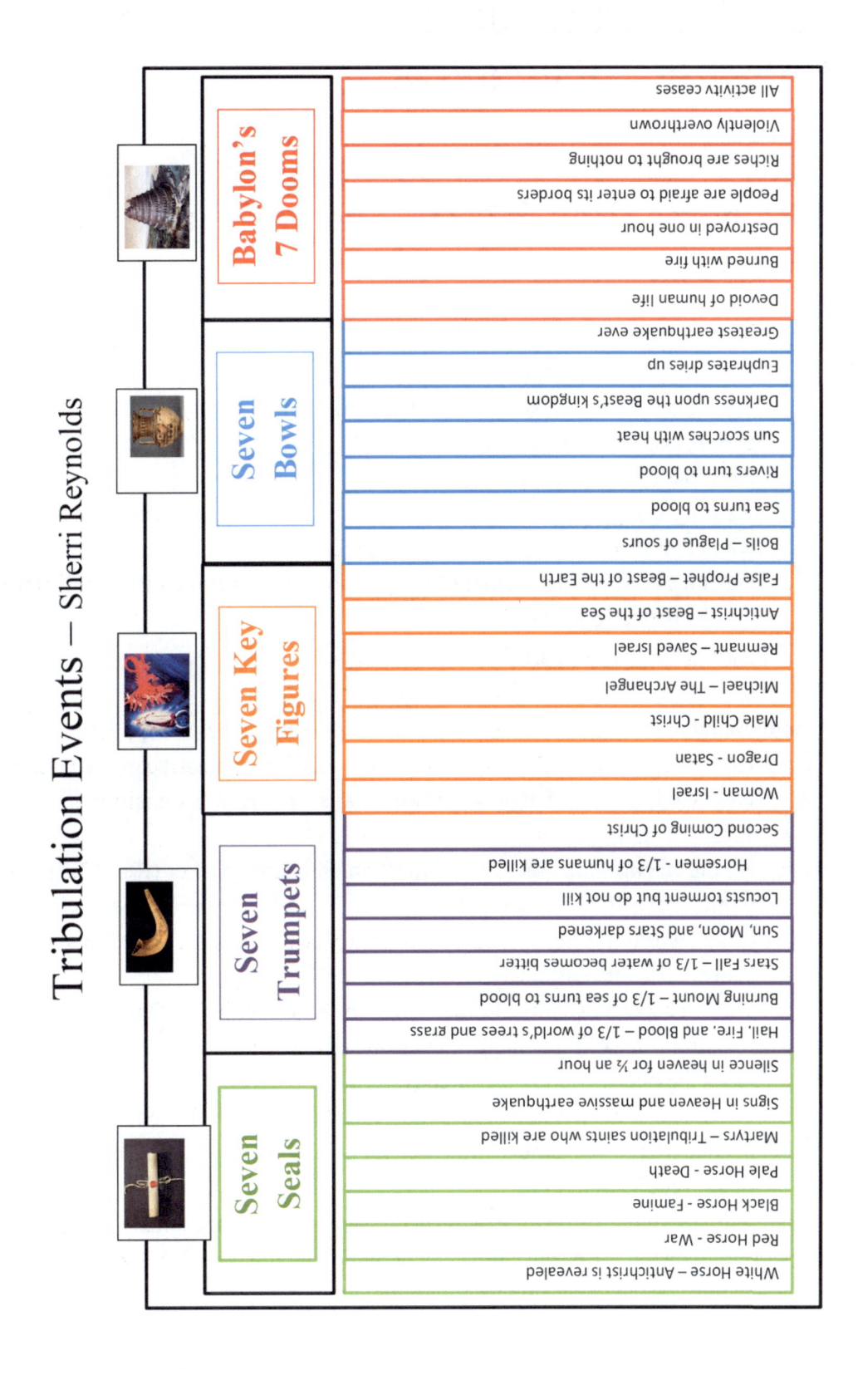

Tribulation Events – Sherri Reynolds

Seven Seals
- White Horse – Antichrist is revealed
- Red Horse - War
- Black Horse - Famine
- Pale Horse - Death
- Martyrs – Tribulation saints who are killed
- Signs in Heaven and massive earthquake
- Silence in heaven for ½ an hour

Seven Trumpets
- Hail, Fire, and Blood – 1/3 of world's trees and grass
- Burning Mount – 1/3 of sea turns to blood
- Stars Fall – 1/3 of water becomes bitter
- Sun, Moon, and Stars darkened
- Locusts torment but do not kill
- Horsemen - 1/3 of humans are killed
- Second Coming of Christ

Seven Key Figures
- Woman - Israel
- Dragon - Satan
- Male Child - Christ
- Michael – The Archangel
- Remnant – Saved Israel
- Antichrist – Beast of the Sea
- False Prophet – Beast of the Earth

Seven Bowls
- Boils – Plague of sours
- Sea turns to blood
- Rivers turn to blood
- Sun scorches with heat
- Darkness upon the Beast's kingdom
- Euphrates dries up
- Greatest earthquake ever

Babylon's 7 Dooms
- Devoid of human life
- Burned with fire
- Destroyed in one hour
- People are afraid to enter its borders
- Riches are brought to nothing
- Violently overthrown
- All activity ceases

The Seven Seal Judgements – First 21 months of the Tribulation – Rev 6:1-8:1.

1. White horse (Rev 6:1-2) - The antichrist is revealed (Dan 9:26-27).

- This does not happen until <u>after</u> the Rapture – II Thess 2:7-8.
    - The white horse symbolizes <u>victory</u> and conquest in war, the bow in hand, but no arrow, is military power through peaceful diplomacy, and the crown is a conquerors crown, not a ruler's crown – Rev 6:2.
    - He is the <u>counterfeit</u> to Jesus.
    - He is a male <u>Gentile</u> - Rev 13:1 "out of the Sea" (Gentile nations, sea of humanity) who comes to establish peace with Israel.
    - He comes out of the last Gentile world power, the revived Roman Empire (EU) and will be its <u>leader</u> – Dan 7:8.
- The 7 heads are 7 <u>emperors</u> of Rome – Rev 13:1.
- The 10 Horns are 10 <u>leaders</u> of Rome – Rev 13:1, Dan 7:7
- Among many other reasons, he is a <u>false</u> Messiah because he is not a Jew.
    - He will do as he wants, exalts and magnifies himself above every god, even the Most High God, just like <u>Satan</u> did when he was cast from his position in heaven – Dan 11:36-37, Is 14:13-14.
    - He blasphemes the One True God, is an eloquent speaker (Rev 13:5), does not desire <u>women</u> (Dan 11:37), is attractive, has an intimidating presence, and will take control of this world politically and economically to begin with, and then about Mid Trib he also takes over religiously.
    - He will cleverly subdue 3 other kings (military genius) – Dan 7:24 - while the remaining 7 willingly <u>submit</u>, leads the one world economy (economic genius), and leads the one world false church (religious).
    - The EU will be in place <u>before</u> the peace treaty is confirmed. Some believe he is headquartered in Rome (7 hilled city). Others believe he will be headquartered in a literal rebuilt Babylon.
- The antichrist will take already <u>established</u> peace treaties with Israel and confirm them for 7 years giving Israel a false sense of security, which he breaks after 3 ½ years (Dan 9:27). Israel lets their guard down thinking that they are protected.

2. Red horse (Rev 6:3-4) – open war and bloodshed (Matt 24:6-7).

- This is due to both the antichrist and China expanding their political reach.
  - The antichrist's plan of world dominance meets resistance and war breaks out against him.
  - He is attempting to subdue Islam, its nations, and all allies among others who want to dominate.
- There is a study by David R. Reagan where he suggests a series of nine wars that range in time from potentially right before the Rapture and Tribulation until the end of the Millennium (Reagan, na). It is very interesting, but definitely his opinion.

3. Black horse (Rev 6:5-6).

- Famine – farmers used time and resources for war and starvation kills millions, money has 1/8 of its former buying power, does not affect the rich. It will cost a day's wages for a loaf of bread. If minimum wage is $10, a loaf of bread would cost $80 – Rev 6:6.
- The famine is the effect of the 2 witnesses who have the power to prevent it from raining – Rev 11:6.

4. Pale (green) horse (Rev 6:7-8).

- Called Death and followed by Hell - Death and pestilence, killed by sword, hunger, and beasts.
- God will take away the fear of man from the beasts. The prey will become the predator. Even pets become wild.
- ¼ of earth's population dies. The present population is 8 billion. That will equal 2 billion deaths.

5. Martyrs of the Tribulation saints (Rev 6:9-11).

- 2 out of every 3 Jews are killed (Zech 13:8). The souls are around the base of the altar like the blood from the sacrifices that were offered, crying out to the Lord to be avenged.
- They are given white robes and told to wait a little longer until their fellow servants who are martyred join them.
- 25% of the world's population will be killed in the first 2 years of the Tribulation.

6. Signs in the <u>heavens</u> and a single, great earthquake which is felt around the world (Rev 6:12-17).

- Sun goes dark, moon turns to blood, stars fall, mountains and islands move, the first heaven (atmosphere) and second heaven (space) <u>split</u> and roll back like a scroll that is opened and torn in two down the middle, revealing the third heaven where God is seated on His throne and the wrath of The Lamb!! – Rev 6:14.
- All men on earth hide themselves in caves and rocks of the mountains crying out for them to hide them from the <u>face</u> of God and the wrath of The Lamb.
- Remember that there are 144,000 male Jewish servants of God that are sealed in their foreheads against the <u>wrath</u> of God, 12,000 from each tribe of Israel – Rev 7:2-8.
- There is a great multitude of Tribulation saints, angels, elders, and the 4 living creatures loudly <u>praising</u> God at this point – Rev 7:9-17.

7. Silence in heaven the space of ½ an hour (Rev 8:1).

- The multitudes and angels had just been <u>praising</u> God loudly – Rev 7:9-17.
- During the silence, an angel comes to the <u>altar</u> and offers much incense and all the prayers of the saints.
- Some believe this pause and silence is God's final chance for <u>mercy,</u> to see man's response before He unleashes the 7 Trumpets and 7 Bowl Judgements.
- Seven trumpets are given to <u>angels</u>.
- Trumpet Judgements begin.

The Seven Seals of Revelation

Rev. 6:1-17; 8:1 – Sherri Reynolds

White Horse	Red Horse	Black Horse	Pale Horse	Martyrs	Signs in Heavens	Silence
Antichrist is revealed - 7:2	War – 7:4	Famine - 7:5	Death – 7:7-8	Tribulation saint who are killed 7:9	Sun darkened, Moon turns to blood, earthquake - 7:12	Silence in heaven for ½ an hour – 8:1

The Seven Trumpet Judgements – Rev 8:2-9:21, 11:15-19.

Some place these Trumpets Judgements before the midpoint of the Tribulation. Others place them after the midpoint.

1. Hail, Fire, mixed with Blood – Rev 8:7.
- 1/3 of the world's trees and grass are burned.

2. Burning mountain thrown into the sea – Rev 8:8-9.
- 1/3 of the sea becomes blood, 1/3 of all sea creatures die, 1/3 of ships are destroyed, potentially a mammoth asteroid.

3. Star falls from heaven – Rev 8:10-11.
- Called Wormwood which means bitter, 1/3 of water becomes bitter, 1/3 of rivers and fountains of water become bitter, many die from the drinking water.

4. Sun diminished – Rev 8:12.
- 1/3 of sun, moon, and stars are darkened.

Angel flies through heaven crying "Woe" three times because of the 3 trumpets yet to come – Rev 8:13.

5. Plagues of locusts – Rev 9:1-12.
- **First woe** – Star or angel unlocks the bottomless pit, Abyss.
  - (Luke 8:31 – demons beg Jesus not to command them to go out into the deep or abyss. Demons fear this place).
- A great swarm of demonic locusts are belched up from the bottomless pit.
  - They are to torment but not kill only the humans without the seal of God in their forehead, for 5 months.
  - They are commanded not to hurt any green thing.
  - These alien creatures are like locusts with the face of man, hair of a woman, sound of wings as of chariots going to battle, and tails like scorpions with a stinger – Rev 9:7-10.
  - These are the angels that did not keep their first estate – Jude v.6-7.
- Their leader's name is Abaddon (Hebrew) or Apollyon (Greek) who is "the angel of the bottomless pit" – Rev 9:11.

6. Plague of horsemen – Rev 9:13-21.
- **Second woe** – Loosing of the four angels bound in the Euphrates River.
  - The fact that these angels are bound may indicate that they are evil angels.

- o Unlike the locusts who were given the power to torment, they are given the power to kill – Rev 9:18.
- o According to Scriptures, the Euphrates has always been God's physical division between what is holy (eastern border of the Promised land – Gen 15:18) and what is unholy (kingdoms of Nimrod, Babel, Nineveh, and Babylon – Gen 10:8-11, 11:1-9, Jonah 1:1-4:11, Ezra 5:12).
- 200 million horsemen are released that kill 1/3 of all humans for one year, one day, and one hour.
- Tim LaHaye believed that these horsemen are demonic creatures that come from the bottomless pit (LaHaye, 2001).
- Others believe that they are the armies of China and their allies – North and South.
- 200 million on horseback (alone) – in 1998 China had 2.8 million active soldiers, 1 million reservists, 15 million militia back up for a total of 18.8 million.
- China has 1.2 billion population potential manpower base of another 200 million males fit for military service.
- There is the theory that since China limited their people to one child per family that they aborted the girls so that their one child could be a male to carry on the family name. These armies are killing men to take the women, so they do not become extinct.
- Whether demonic or literal, half of the world (4 billion people) are killed by the midpoint of the Tribulation.
- There is still no repentance from those who are not killed – Rev 9:21.

At this point, there are 7 thunders (Rev 10:1-7), 7 voices of God (Ps 29).

- John was just about to write down what he saw, but a voice from heaven told him to seal up those things which the thunders uttered, and do not write them down.
- These are divine judgements.
- It is easy to just move on in the study because there is nothing revealed in these judgments, but I am sure there is much here since they are sealed up.
- There is then an announcement that there will be no more delay to God revealing His purpose in human history.
- Good and evil are completely revealed.

7. Christ rules – Rev 11:15-19.

- 24 elders saying wrath and judgement have come to the wicked and rewards have come to those that fear the name of God (wrath/reward).
- Vision of the future yet to come.
- 7 vial judgements proceed from this trumpet.
- Some place this last Trumpet at mid-Tribulation. Some believe this Trumpet does not happen until the Second Coming of Christ.

The Seven Trumpets of Revelation

Rev. 8:7-9:21; 11:15-19 – Sherri Reynolds

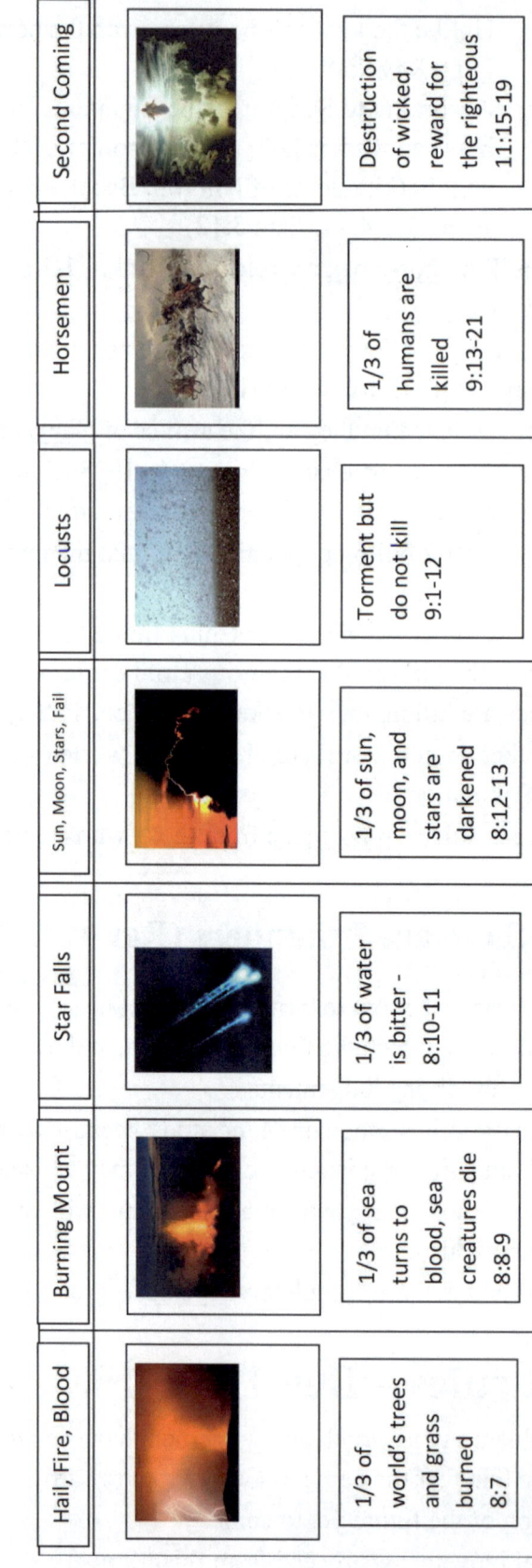

Hail, Fire, Blood	Burning Mount	Star Falls	Sun, Moon, Stars, Fail	Locusts	Horsemen	Second Coming
1/3 of world's trees and grass burned 8:7	1/3 of sea turns to blood, sea creatures die 8:8-9	1/3 of water is bitter - 8:10-11	1/3 of sun, moon, and stars are darkened 8:12-13	Torment but do not kill 9:1-12	1/3 of humans are killed 9:13-21	Destruction of wicked, reward for the righteous 11:15-19

The Seven Key Figures – Rev 12:1-13:18

1. Woman – Rev 12:1-2.
- Nation of Israel, the <u>mother</u> of Christ, the focus of Biblical prophecy once again rests on them during the Tribulation, hid in the wilderness for 3 ½ years, Petra in Jordan – Dan 11:41 (current country of Jordan and the city of Petra), Rev 12:6.

2. Dragon – Rev 12:3-4.
- Satan – counterfeit of <u>The Father</u> and 1/3 of the fallen angels.

3. Male Child – Rev 12:5.
- <u>Christ</u> Who is taken to Heaven.

4. Michael – Rev 12:7-8.
- Archangel and <u>Commander in Chief</u> of the good angels.
- There is a war at the midpoint of the Tribulation between Michael and his angels and the dragon and his angels.

5. Remnant – Rev 12:13-17.
- Jews who are saved <u>during</u> the Tribulation.
- They <u>flee</u> to the wilderness until the return of Christ – Dan 11:41, Hosea 2:14-15, Rev 12:6.

6. Antichrist – Rev 13:1-10.
- Beast of the <u>sea</u> (Gentile nations) – counterfeit of The Son – his power is given to him by Satan – Rev 13:2.
- All unsaved will <u>worship</u> him – Rev 13:8-12.
- He will <u>confirm</u> a treaty with Israel and midway through the Tribulation he will break it – Dan 9:27.
- He will come upon the <u>Jews</u> with crushing power.
- He will be killed and come back to <u>life</u> – Rev 13:3.
- Some think this is <u>literal</u>, others believe that it is the Roman power come back to life.
- It is by Satan's power that he comes back to life (counterfeit of Christ's <u>resurrection</u>).
- There will be many new <u>converts</u> during the Tribulation, but he will mercilessly torture and kill them – Rev 13:7.
- He will have <u>power</u> over the world for 3 ½ years – Rev 13:5.

7. False Prophet – Rev 13:11-18.
- Beast of the <u>earth</u> (particular nation or location) – counterfeit of The Holy Spirit – The antichrist's associate.

- <u>Appears</u> religious - Rev 13:12, and looks harmless like a lamb – Rev 13:11.
- He is the <u>leader</u> of the one world religion (one god under many names, worship any god you like – freedom religion) – Rev 13:12.
- This false church will be built on the <u>remnants</u> of the non-professing church, its power will be enhanced by political alliances made by the antichrist.
- Some believe the false prophet will be the <u>Pope</u> who rules in Rome at the Vatican. The word "Pope" is short for Pontifus Maximus referring to the Roman Caesars.
- All of the Caesar's religious responsibilities are traced back to Babylon and the Tower of Babel. <u>Nimrod</u> was the ruler (Gen 10:8-11). Nimrod, his wife Semiramis, and their son Tammuz founded their own religion (making themselves all deity) which was, many centuries later, integrated into Christianity through the Roman Catholic church. That is where we get the Catholics making Mary deity.
- The Roman Catholic church is the <u>false</u> counterfeit of Christ's church.
- The number of this beast is <u>666</u> – Rev 13:18.
- The pope's official mitre (<u>headdress</u>) is "Vicarius Filii Dei" which means "Vicar (representative) of the son of God". V=5, I=1, C=100, A=no value, R=no value, I=1, U/V=5, S=no value, F=no value, I=1, L=50, I-1, I=1, D=500, E=no value, I=1 for a total of 666.
- Naman believes that 666 represents the number of the man which closely <u>represents</u> King Nebuchadnezzar who built a statute 60 cubit high, 6 cubits wide, and was heralded by 6 musical instruments. Everyone was commanded to bow down and worship it (Dan 3:2-7). The first 6 represents the number of man. The second and third 6 represents the dimension of the statute (Naman, 2021). The false prophet also erects a statue of the antichrist and commands everyone to bow down and worship it – Rev 13:15.
- He does signs, wonders, and miracles to <u>deceive</u> the world and betray the church – Rev 13:13-18.
- The false prophet makes an image of the Beast and <u>empowers</u> the image with life and speech – Rev 13:15.
    - He causes all to receive the mark of the Beast and <u>worship</u> the Beast in order to buy and sell – Rev 13:16-17.
    - The purpose of the mark is to <u>control</u> financial transactions and economic commerce – Rev 13:15-18.
    - Those who <u>do not</u> worship the image will be put to death – Rev 13:15.
    - Those who do receive the mark and worship the beast are eventually thrown into the <u>Lake of fire</u> – Rev 14:9-11.

Seven Figures of Revelation

(Rev 12 & 13) – Sherri Reynolds

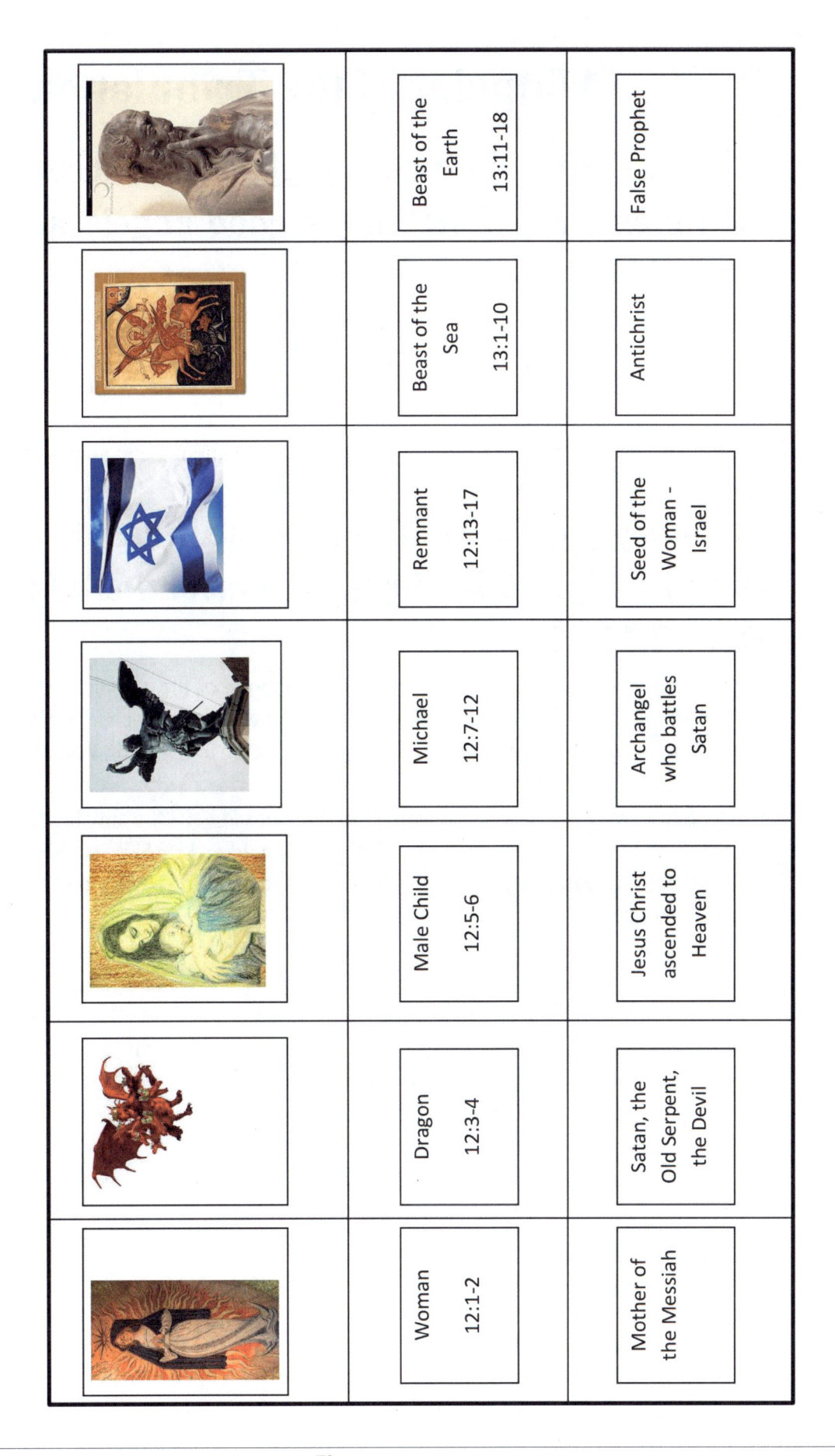

Woman 12:1-2	Dragon 12:3-4	Male Child 12:5-6	Michael 12:7-12	Remnant 12:13-17	Beast of the Sea 13:1-10	Beast of the Earth 13:11-18
Mother of the Messiah	Satan, the Old Serpent, the Devil	Jesus Christ ascended to Heaven	Archangel who battles Satan	Seed of the Woman - Israel	Antichrist	False Prophet

Midpoint of the Tribulation

- **War in Heaven between <u>Michael</u> the Archangel, Commander in Chief of the good angels, and Satan with his evil angels – Rev 12:7-12.**
    - When Satan fell at the beginning, he fell from his <u>position</u> in heaven.
    - He still has <u>access</u> to the Throne and presence of God (Job 1:6) where he accuses the brethren day and night (Rev 12:10) until this point when he and his angels war against Michael and his army and fail.
    - They are cast out of Heaven <u>permanently</u>. Satan and his evil angels are thrown out of heaven forever and, at this point, cast down to the earth – Rev 12:9, 12.
- **Satan's <u>anger</u> intensifies after he is cast from heaven (Rev 12:12) and he turns to persecution of the Jews – Rev 12:13-17.**
    - "Religious Babylon" is destroyed at the midpoint of the Tribulation. The antichrist now has full <u>worship</u> of the world with the false prophet as his associate. Because of the peace treaty and the great victory he claims from the first Gog and Magog war, the Jews receive the antichrist eagerly.
    - Satan, who now resides on <u>earth</u> (Rev 12:12), indwells the antichrist, stops temple sacrifices (Dan 11:31), and desecrates the Temple (Dan 9:27, 11:31) by standing in the Holy of Holies (Matt 24:15), sitting down (II Thess 2:4), and claiming to be God (Abomination of Desolation).
    - The false prophet puts a statue of the <u>Beast</u> in the Holy of Holies and makes people worship it – Rev 13:14.
    - He <u>empowers</u> it to live and speak – Rev 13:15.
    - The mark of the Beast is <u>required</u> at this point (like a credit card) in order to buy and sell as a sign of worship and allegiance to the antichrist – Rev 13:15-17.
    - Those who take the mark will be eternally punished in the Lake of Fire – Rev 14:9-11, 20:15.
    - Jews will become disillusioned with the <u>antichrist</u>.
    - The Lord will take away their heart of <u>stone</u> and they return to their Messiah – Ez 11:19-20.
    - Satan and his evil angels attempt to wipe out Israel, so God is unable to keep His <u>promise</u> to the Jewish people – Rev 12:13.
    - The people of Israel <u>flee</u>.
    - <u>Michael</u> is instructed by God to protect His people (Dan 12:1). They are protected, preserved, and nourished in the wilderness (Petra, Jordan) for 3 ½ years – Rev 12:6.
    - Satan tries to destroy them by <u>flood</u>, but the earth opens up and swallows the flood – Rev 12:15-16.

- **The political Babylon will destroy the religious Babylon – Rev 17:1-13.**
    - The antichrist is the <u>only</u> object of worship – Rev 13:4, 15.
    - Political Babylon will be destroyed by <u>Christ</u> at Armageddon – Rev 19:20.

- **The two witnesses who preached for 3 ½ years are killed by the antichrist and left to rot in the <u>streets</u> for 3 ½ days – Rev 11:3-14.**
    - The whole world throws a <u>party</u> and gives gifts to one another because these witnesses were given the ability to rain down fire, prevent it from raining which contributed to famines, and kill those who mocked them – Rev 11:8-11.
    - After the 3½ days the two witnesses are resurrected and raptured to heaven while the world is <u>watching</u> – Rev 11:12.
    - Even though the <u>supply chains</u> are broken, satellites still work so everyone around the world can still see this event.
    - A great earthquake will destroy 1/10 of <u>Jerusalem</u> killing 7,000 people – Rev 11:13.
    - Many <u>repent</u> and glorify God. As a result, the antichrist will be emboldened to retaliate on the nation of Israel worse than the Holocaust.

- **Result of the preaching of the 144,000 witnesses**
    - There are many saved in the <u>second</u> half of the Tribulation.

- **An <u>angel</u> is sent to proclaim the Gospel**
    - Warned to give glory to God only, and not to take the <u>mark</u> of the beast or they will face eternal flames – Rev 14:6.
    - He takes this message to every nation, tribe, tongue, and people. "These from all <u>nations</u> are the saved who came from the tribulation" – Rev 7:9.

NOTES

CHAPTER 9

What Happens on Earth – Last 3 ½ Years

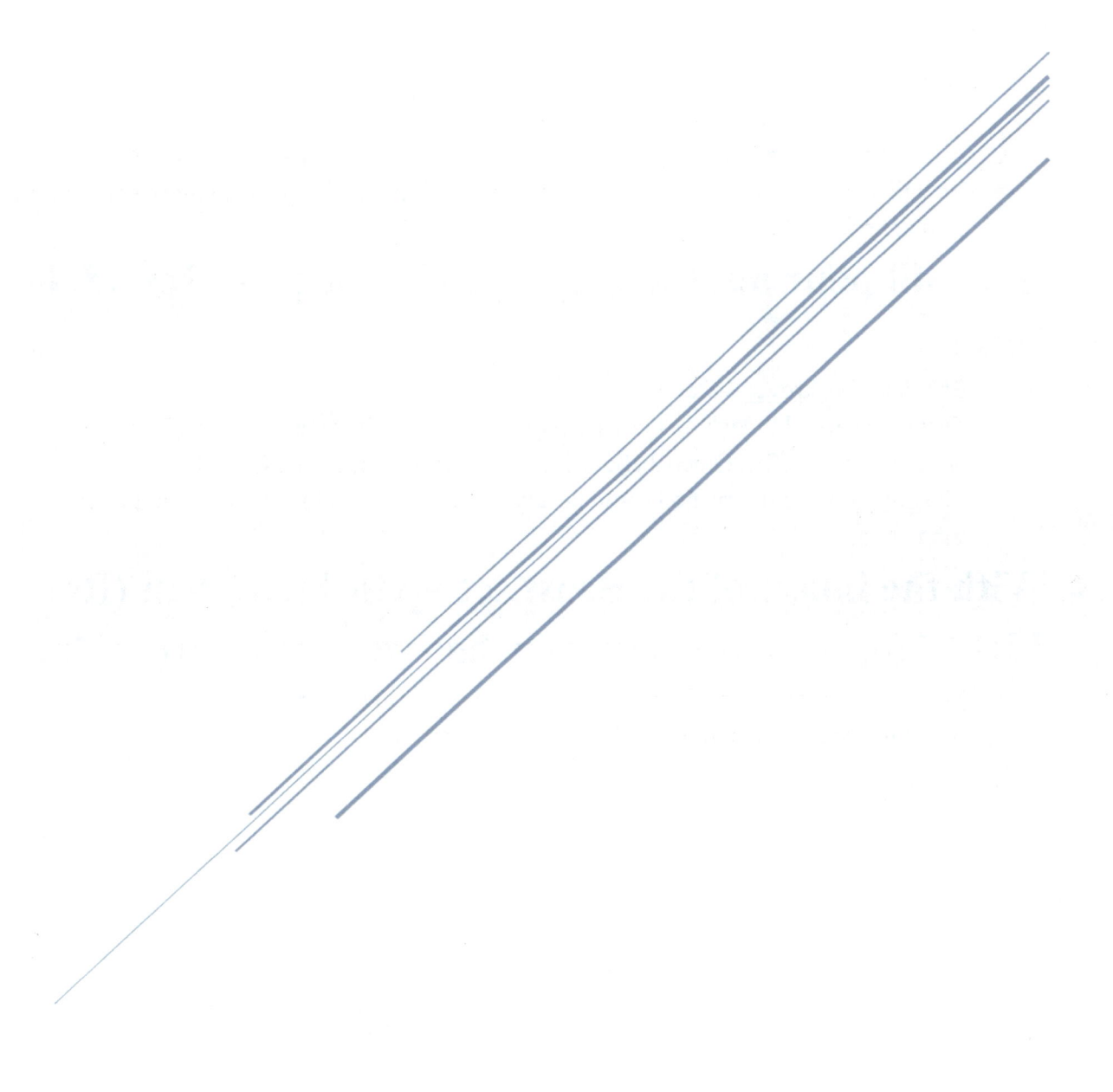

Last 3 ½ Years of the Tribulation

- **The "Great Tribulation" – Matt 24:21.**
    - The most intense and severe of the <u>judgements</u> and also the most severe persecution of the Jews – Rev 12:13.

- **The antichrist will break his <u>treaty</u> with Israel – Dan 9:27.**
    - Satan, who was cast to earth after the war in heaven, will now <u>indwell</u> the Antichrist and strongly persecute and kill the Jews.
    - A remnant escapes to <u>Jordan</u> where the ancient city of Petra is – Dan 11:41, Rev 12:14.
    - He will also war against "the <u>offspring</u> of Israel" (Rev 12:17), who are those saved during the Tribulation.

- **God will pour out the 7 <u>Bowl</u> Judgements – Rev 15:1-16:21.**
    - Babylon is <u>destroyed</u> – Rev 18.
    - There are several thoughts as to who Babylon is. Some believe it is <u>literal</u> Babylon. Some believe it is the USA. Others believe it is Rome and the Catholic Church.
    - The <u>timing</u> of the destruction could be anywhere between mid-tribulation and later tribulation.

- **With the image of the Beast set up in Jerusalem (Rev 13:14-15), the antichrist now has worldwide worship.**
    - The last 3 ½ years of the Tribulation his <u>focus</u> is turned to domination of the one world economy, one world politics, and one world government.

The Seven Bowl (Pitcher, Pot, Vial) Judgements – Rev 15:1-16:21

The Wrath of God is poured out on the earth. God is <u>alone</u> in His Temple when His wrath is poured out (Rev 15:7-8). The bowls are emptied out completely.

1. **Boils, plague of terrible sours – Rev 16:1-2.**
   - Upon all those who <u>denied</u> Christ, did not receive Him but rejected Him and took the mark of the Beast, and believed a lie.

2. **Sea turns to blood – Rev 16:3.**
   - All <u>sea</u> life dies. Stench and disease result.

3. **Rivers and fountains of water turn to blood – Rev 16:4-7**
   - All <u>fresh</u> water turns to blood. All water life dies. There is now no fresh drinking water.

4. **Great heat, Sun scorches the earth – Rev 16:8-9.**
   - Men are scorched with great <u>heat</u>.
   - Remember there is no fresh <u>drinking</u> water from the previous Bowl.
   - People <u>still</u> blaspheme God and refuse to repent of their sins.

5. **Beast's kingdom is darkened and brings <u>agony</u> (poured out on the throne of the Beast) – Rev 16:10-11.**
   - All <u>land</u> claimed by the Beast will be darkened and men will blaspheme God because of their pain.

6. **Euphrates River dries up – Rev 16:12.**
   - The Euphrates dries up so that China, India, and the other <u>eastern</u> nations can make their way to battle at Armageddon.
   - Satan, antichrist, and the false prophet call for all the armies of the world to <u>join</u> and fight against the returning Messiah at Armageddon – Rev 16:13-16.

7. **God's <u>voice</u> from His Temple (Rev 16:17-21) poured out into the air, upon the prince of the power of the air, saying "It is Finished".**
   - God's <u>wrath</u> – Storms, lightning, thunder, and the greatest earthquake like never before recorded, flattens cites and mountains, and islands will disappear.
   - It destroys Babylon (literal, Rome or USA), with hail 50-100 lbs, splits into three. God destroys it in one hour. People <u>harden</u> their hearts against God further.

The Seven Bowls of Revelation

Rev. 16:1-21 – Sherri Reynolds

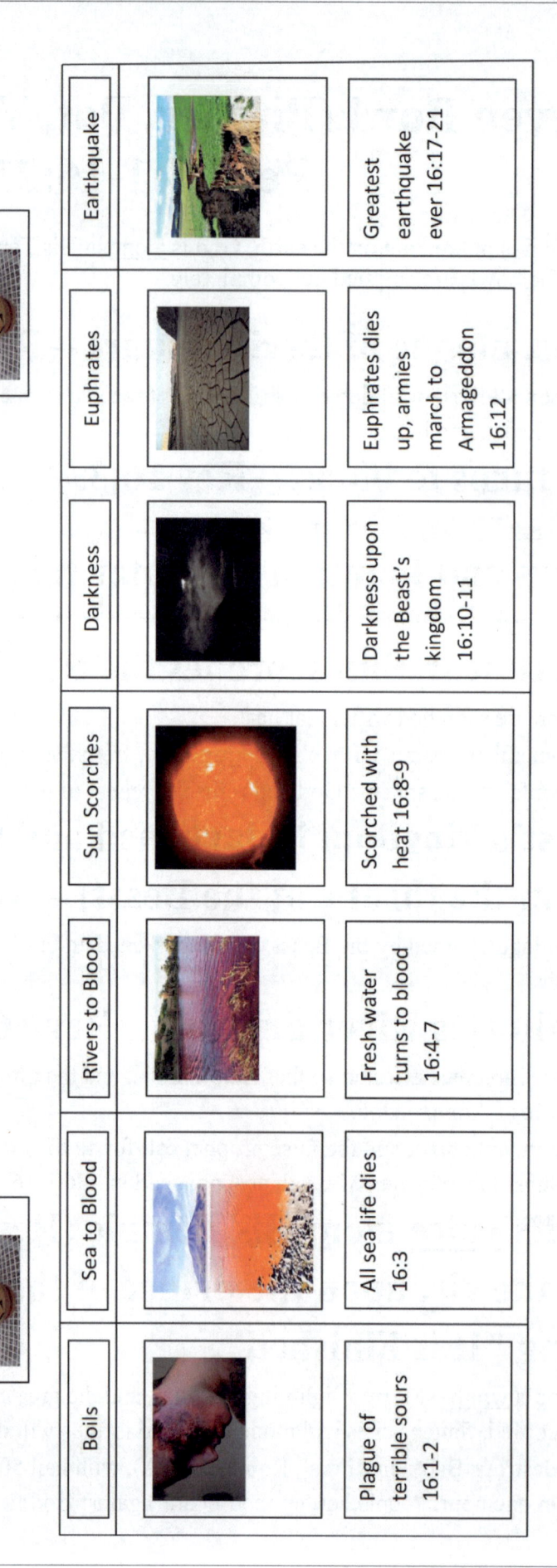

Boils	Sea to Blood	Rivers to Blood	Sun Scorches	Darkness	Euphrates	Earthquake
Plague of terrible sours 16:1-2	All sea life dies 16:3	Fresh water turns to blood 16:4-7	Scorched with heat 16:8-9	Darkness upon the Beast's kingdom 16:10-11	Euphrates dies up, armies march to Armageddon 16:12	Greatest earthquake ever 16:17-21

Dooms of Babylon (Fall of literal Babylon, Rome, or the USA) – Rev 17:1-18:24.

- The Great Whore whom the <u>kings</u> of the earth have committed fornication and made drunk with her wine, arrayed in scarlet, purple, gold, and precious stones and pearls, with a golden cup full of abominations, and drunk with the blood of the saints and martyrs of Jesus, sitting on a scarlet beast, who was, is not, and yet is, full of names of blasphemy.
- The whore is one who <u>loved</u> God and left Him.
- There are theories as to who she is.
    - It could be a <u>literal</u> Babylon which is yet to come to this kind of power.
    - It could be the <u>religious</u> system that grows out of Babylon (Roman Catholicism being used by the False Prophet to form a one world religion).
        - Becomes <u>powerful,</u> and she rides the beast which is the governmental system (EU, 10 nations, led by the antichrist, beast with 10 horns).
        - She is arrayed in the <u>colors</u> of a Roman Catholic priest in full garb.
        - They work <u>together</u> until mid-Tribulation when she is destroyed by the kings of the earth – Rev 17.
        - The False prophet seizes this opportunity and gets people to worship the antichrist who is now <u>indwelt</u> by Satan.
    - It could be the USA.
        - Most nations have <u>traded</u> with the USA, and some have become very rich.
        - The political and economic side will be headed by the antichrist which is controlled by the USA from the <u>United Nations</u>.
        - The antichrist and 10 nations are the EU which will be global <u>partners</u> with the USA.
        - For the first 3 ½ years of the Tribulation, the <u>USA</u> will control the antichrist and 10 nation confederacy.
        - When Satan indwells the antichrist halfway through the Tribulation, he and his allies will <u>turn</u> on the USA with a nuclear attack.
        - The USA will be completely destroyed and <u>uninhabitable</u>.
        - The defeat is <u>swift,</u> in one hour.
        - There will be a dramatic change in <u>power</u> and the antichrist will take over the one world economy and government.
- Description of the destruction of Babylon.
    - Devoid of <u>human</u> life.
    - Burned with <u>fire</u>.
    - Destroyed in <u>one</u> hour – Rev 18:17.
    - People afraid to enter her borders, the merchants of the earth will lament and mourn her destruction. They will watch her <u>burn</u> from afar off – Rev 18:15.

- o <u>Riches</u> brought to nothing.
- o <u>Violently</u> overthrown.
- o All activity <u>ceases</u>.
- After the fall of Babylon, the antichrist takes over complete political, economic, governmental, and religious control of the <u>world</u>.
  - o He will march into the Temple in Jerusalem, sit down in The <u>Holy of Holies</u>, and demand worldwide worship – Dan 9:27, 11:31; Matt 24:15; II Thess 2:4.
  - o The <u>Jews</u> will turn on him and assassinate him – Rev 13:3.
  - o He will come back to life counterfeiting the <u>resurrection</u> of Christ – Rev 13:2-6.
  - o At this point, he will initiate a mass Jewish execution, and they flee to the wilderness, some believe it will be <u>Petra</u> in Jordan – Dan 11:41; Rev 12:6, 13-14.
- The False Prophet will set up an image of the antichrist in The Holy of Holies, gives it <u>power</u> to live and speak, demanding that all worship it – Rev 13:14-15.
  - o He will also force people to take the mark of the beast in order to <u>buy</u> and sell – Rev 13:17.
  - o He will <u>kill</u> those who do not take the mark – Rev 20:4.
- The Marriage Supper of the Lamb takes place in heaven toward the end of the Tribulation – Rev 19:7-9.
  - o Some believe it will not take place until <u>after</u> the Second Coming but before the Millennium.
  - o John places the Marriage Supper of the Lamb in Rev 19:7-10, which chronologically comes <u>before</u> his writing on the Second Coming of Christ in Rev 19:11-16.

CHAPTER 10

The Second Coming of Christ

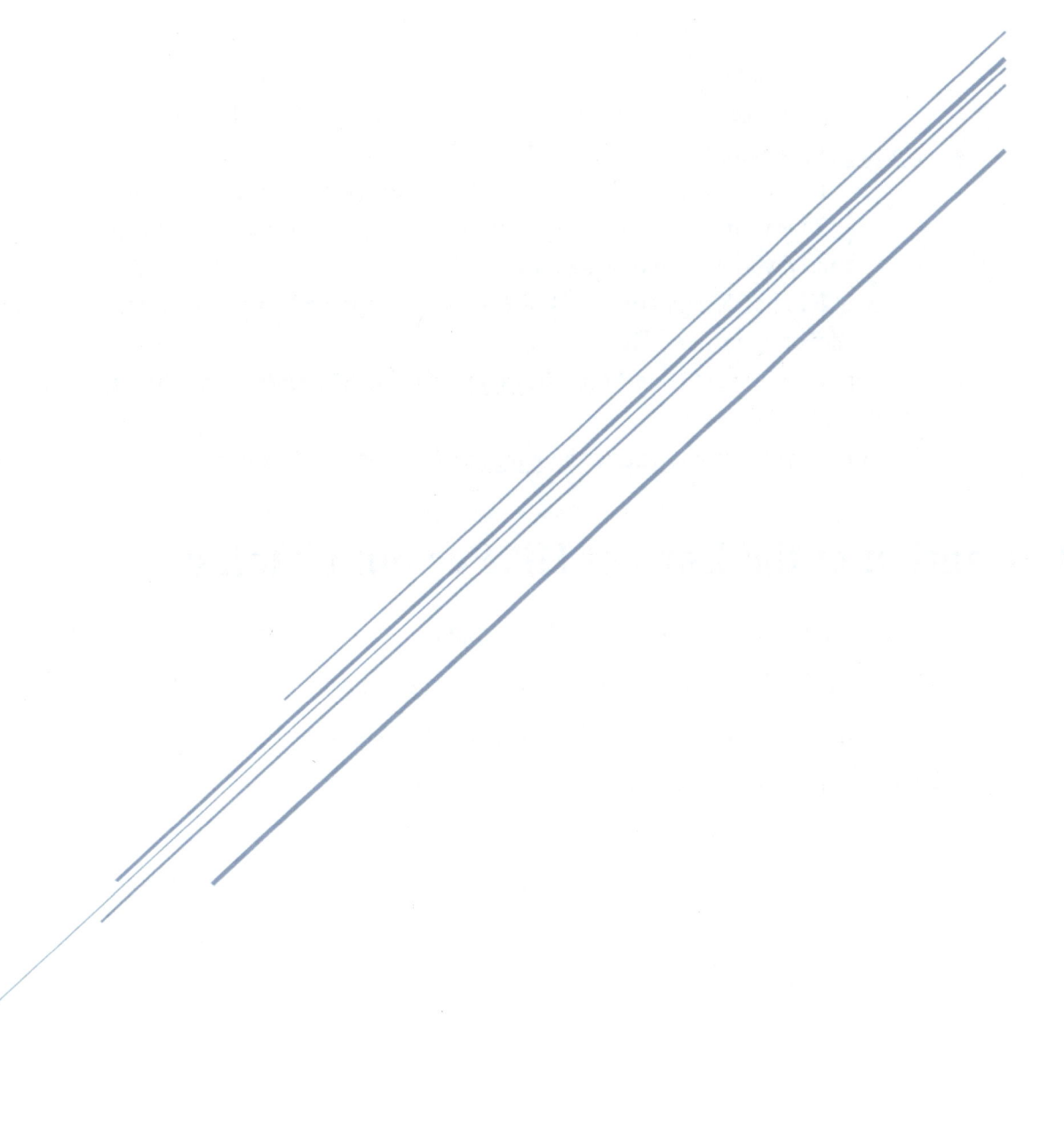

The Second Coming of Christ

Return of the King of kings and Lord of lords as the Righteous Warrior

(Rev 19:11-15)

- **The Bride of Christ has made herself ready through the Bema Seat Judgement – Rev 19:7-8.**
    - They are now purified and wearing robes of white – Rev 19:14.
- **Like a Galilean wedding, the day and hour of His second coming, no man knows.**
    - Only the Father knows – Matt 24:36.
- **A sign will appear of the Son of Man in heaven and then He will return.**
    - Immediately after the Tribulation there will be major changes in the sky and then the sign of the Son of Man will appear in heaven – Matt 24:29-31.
- **Names He is called** – Rev 19:11-13, 16:
    - **"Faithful and True"** – our Lord's dignity as the Eternal Son – Rev 19:11.
    - **"The Word of God"** – Incarnation, coming to earth to die for your sins, became flesh and dwelt among us – Rev 19:13.
    - **"King of Kings and Lord of Lords"** – second advent. Coming to reign, majestic, sovereign ruler – Rev 19:16.
- **The nation of Israel is gathered in belief of their Messiah, a spiritual gathering** – Ez 39:29, Jer 33:16.
- **The Lord will come to judge the earth at His Second Coming** – Ps 98:9.

Description of the Lord at His Second Coming

- Descending from the heavens on a white horse, the heavens will open – Rev 19:11.
- Eyes – Flame of fire. Pierce and judge the motives of nations and individuals – Rev 19:12.
- Head – Crowned with many crowns, absolute authority – Rev 19:12.
- Robe – Dipped in blood – sacrificial Lamb – Rev 19:13.
- Mouth – Sharp sword to smite the nations – Rev 11:15.
- Vesture and thigh – Name written: KING OF KINGS, AND LORD OF LORDS – Rev 11:16.
- In some places of the world, it will be day and in other places it will be night – Luke 17:34-36.
- Great sound of a trumpet – Matt 24:31.

Returning with <u>Armies</u> of Christ

- Returning with tens of thousands of His <u>saints</u>, - OT, NT, Trib saints – Zech 14:5, I Thess 3:13, II Thess 1:10.
- Riding on white horses, dressed in fine <u>linen</u> white and clean – Rev 19:14.
  - Soldiers usually wear <u>dark</u> clothing or camouflage, not white because they do not expect their clothing to remain clean.
  - Christ's army will wear white because they will never actually <u>fight</u>.
  - <u>God</u> does it all – Rev 19:21.
- Returning with all (thousands and millions) of His <u>angels</u> – Matt 25:31.
- God's longsuffering <u>patience</u> will have run its course – Rev 11:18

Physical Changes

- Immediately <u>after</u> the Tribulation, the sun, moon, and stars go dark – Matt 24:29.
- The Glory of God and the Lamb are the <u>light</u> – Rev 21:23.
- The borders of Israel will expand to the <u>original</u> promised land – Ez 47:13-48:29.
- There will be <u>portions</u> for the Levites, priests, and princes – Ez 48:10-22.

Reshaping of Jerusalem – Is 2:2, Zech 14:4-5, Mic 4:2

- Christ will touch down on the <u>Mount of Olives</u> and it will split in half east to west so that the Mt. of Olives moves north to south with a great valley between – Zech 14:4-5.
- In 1964, a <u>fault</u> line was discovered on the Mount of Olives.
- Land set aside with <u>Temple</u> in the midst – 42.5 miles by 17 miles – Ez 48:8-9.
- Description and measurements of the <u>Millennial</u> Temple – Ez 40:5-42:20.
- The Temple will be built <u>while</u> the armies are making their way to the Jezreel Valley.

The Avenging Christ

- Reclaiming the <u>title</u> deed of the earth from Satan and cleansing, purging.
- He is given His <u>throne</u> back – Dan 7:13-14.

Armageddon

- Hebrew for "the mount of Megiddo", "the mount of slaughter" – Rev 16:13-16; 19:17-19.
- Place – Located in northern Israel. It is an extended plain from the Mediterranean Sea to northern part of Israel known as the Jezreel Valley.
    - More than 200 battles have been fought here including Crusaders, Egyptians, Persians, Greeks, Turks, and Arabs.
    - The armies of the nations will gather in the valley of Armageddon – Rev 19:19.
- Purpose
    - To finish His judgement on Israel – "Time of Jacob's trouble" – Jer 30:7.
    - To finalize His judgment upon the nations that have persecuted Israel – Joel 3:2, Zeph 3:15.
    - To formally judge all the nations that have rejected Him – Joel 3:12-14, Rev 19:11, 15.
- The Battle - Will include all nations of the world – Rev 16:14.
    - They will come from the north, south, east, and west.
    - They are led by the antichrist – Rev 19:19.
- These events are inspired and directed by the demons of hell – Rev 16:14.
- Satan may finance the final battle with money he generated from the Garden of Eden, which he spoiled at the beginning, now buried, and turned into oil.
- All the kings and armies will be defeated by The Word of Christ (Roar of The Lion of Judah) – Is 66:15-16, Rev 19:15, 21.
- The Beast and the false prophet are immediately cast into the Lake of Fire – Rev 19:20.
    - God simply flings them alive into the Lake of Fire where they are still alive 1,000 years later – Rev 20:10.
    - The Lake of Fire is neither annihilation nor purgatory where you pay off your debt.
- The blood will flow as high as a horse's bridle (4 ft) for 200 miles – Rev 14:20.
- The dead will lie where they fell and are consumed by scavenger birds (The Feast of the birds), supper of the Great God – Jer 25:33, Rev 19:17-18, 21.

After Armageddon

- All unsaved humans on the earth will be slain by the sword which proceeds from the <u>mouth</u> of Him Who sits on the horse – Rev 19:21.
    - There will be no unsaved humans who <u>enter</u> the millennium.
- Separation of the sheep (saved saints who survived the Tribulation) and goats (unsaved Tribulation survivors), the "brethren" in this passage refers to the <u>saved</u> Jews – Matt 25:31-46.
    - Every individual from <u>all</u> nations will be judged – Matt 25:32.
    - <u>Believers</u> will be involved as judges of both men and angels – I Cor 6:2-3.
    - The <u>goats</u> are killed and cast into torment until the end of the Millennium, and eventually into the Lake of Fire after the White Throne Judgement along with all other unbelievers – Matt 25:41, Rev 20:11-15.
- There are two reapings – Rev 14:14-20.

1. **The first reaper is The <u>Son</u> of Man** – harvests martyred Tribulation believers – Rev 14:15.
    - This is part of the <u>first</u> resurrection.
    - It is a resurrection of the just who were beheaded, killed, or died during the Tribulation.
    - They are judged and <u>reign</u> with Christ 1,000 years – Rev 20:4.
    - Some believe that <u>OT</u> saints are resurrected here – Dan 12:2.
    - Others believe that the OT saints are resurrected at the <u>Rapture</u>.
    - These saints will have the privilege of <u>judging</u> others (unsaved).

2. **The second reaper is an <u>angel</u>** – harvests unbelievers and casts them into the wine press of the wrath of God which is Armageddon – Rev 14:19.
    - The blood was unto the horse's bridle (4 ft), <u>200</u> miles long – Rev 14:20.
    - Satan is bound by an angel and thrown into a bottomless pit for 1,000 years – Rev 20:1-3.
    - Interesting that one angel of God has <u>more</u> power than Satan.
    - The first three chapters and last three chapters of the Bible are the only ones when <u>Satan</u> is not in control.
    - The fallen angels are cast to hell and delivered to chains of darkness – II Pet 2:4, Jude v.6.

- <u>God</u> simply snatches up the antichrist and the false prophet and flings them alive into the Lake of Fire – Rev 19:20.
    - They will still be <u>alive</u> 1,000 years later – Rev 20:10.

- Satan is bound and thrown into a bottomless pit for the Millennium – Rev 20:1-2.
- Satan is loosed after the Millenium for a short time when he rises up for a <u>last</u> rebellion – Rev 20:7.
- God casts Satan into The Lake of Fire after the Millennium where he will dwell permanently for the rest of <u>eternity</u> – Rev 20:10.
- The Lake of Fire is neither annihilation nor purgatory where you pay off your debt. It is <u>eternal</u> – Rev 20:10.

75 Day Interval – Dan 12:11-12

- Could <u>potentially</u> happen toward the end of the Tribulation right before the Second Coming, or between the Second Coming and the Millennium.
- The atmospheric heaven and the earth are destroyed by <u>fire</u> as the flood in the days of Noah – Is 65:17, II Pet 3:4-13.
- It is <u>purged</u> not done away with.

Second half of Daniel's 70th week, second half of the Tribulation – 1260 days – Dan 12:7.

+30 days – 1290 days – Dan 12:11.

- Cleansing of the <u>Temple</u>, set up the Millennial Temple, purifying of earth and atmospheric heaven, much of the globe has been destroyed.
- Christ will <u>renovate</u> His creation – Ez 40-48.

+45 days – 1335 days – Dan 12:12.

- Judgement of the <u>nations</u>.

----

75 Days Total

- The second gathering of Israel this time in <u>belief</u> – Ez 39:29.
- Restoration of Israel – regeneration, regathering, possession of the <u>entire</u> promised land, re-establishment of the Davidic throne, reign of Jesus Christ – Ez 47:13-48:29.
- Tribulation believers who have died will be given resurrected bodies at the end of the Tribulation.

CHAPTER 11

The Millennium

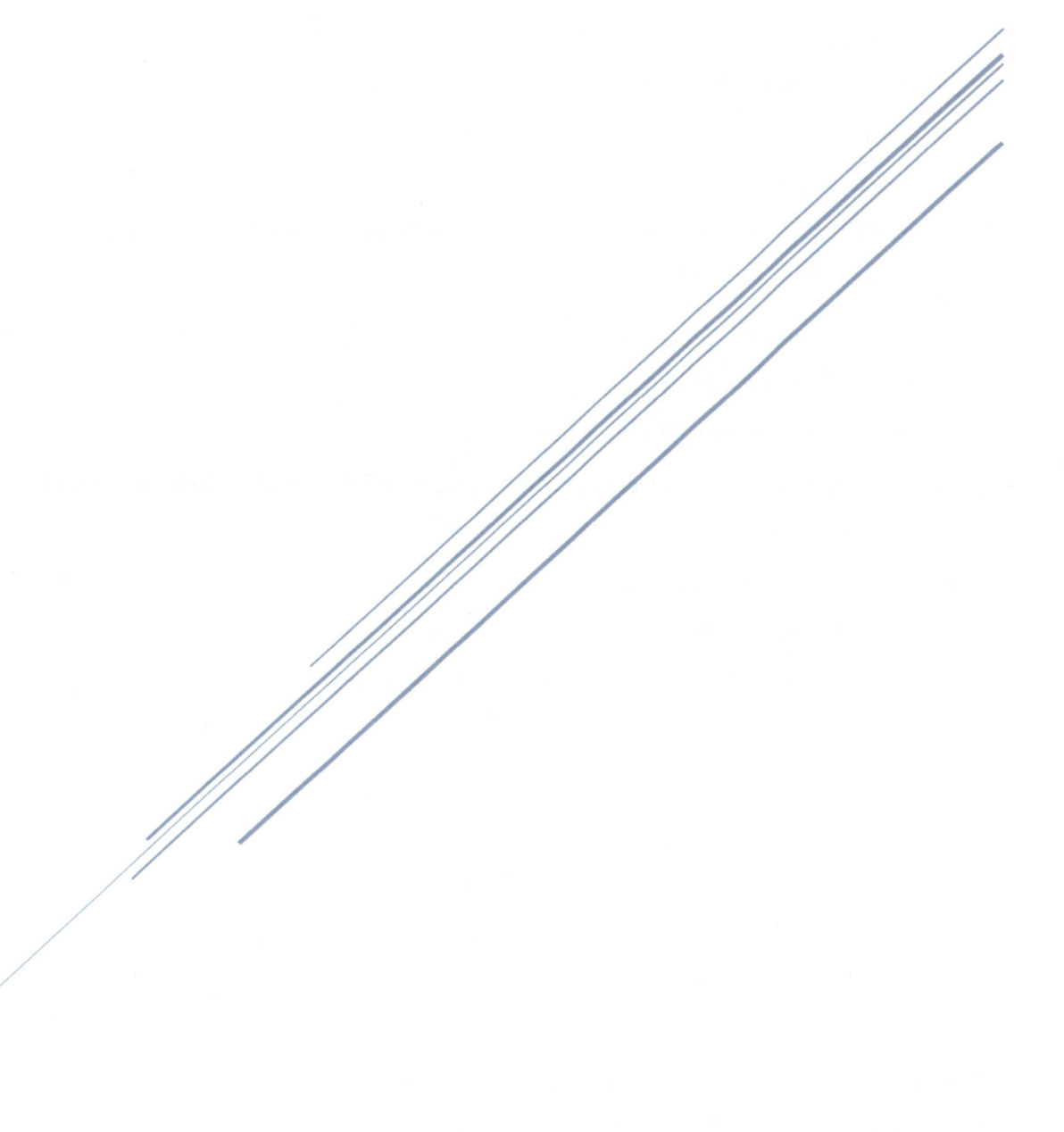

The Millennium

- God will reconcile Israel to Himself, and they are given a special role in the Millennium.
    - David will be the vice-regent over Israel – Ez 34:23-24, 37:24-25; Jer 30:9.
- Israel will be given their full land promised and fulfill her destiny (Ez 37:25), and everlasting covenant of peace with Israel – Ez 34:25, 37:26.
    - God will write His law on their hearts and be their God – Jer 31:33.
- The earth is cleansed and reclaimed.
    - It is released from its curse – Rev 22:3, Rom 8:21-22.
    - There is a regeneration – "genesis again" – Is 51:3, II Pet 3:10-12.
    - Potentially "elements shall melt" – dissolved by fire.
    - It will be like at creation.
- Rebellion will still exist, but it will be rooted out and punished swiftly – Is 2:4, Mic 4:3, Rev 19:15.
- Physical bodied believers that survived the Tribulation will move into the Millennium.
    - Separation of the sheep (physical bodied believers) and goats (physical bodied unbelievers) who are taken away to everlasting punishment - Matt 25:31-46.
- These believers will be both Jew and Gentile.
- The Holy Spirit will once again indwell the believers and their bodies will be renewed as in their youth, no disease, etc. – Is 65:20.
- Tribulation believers who have died will be given resurrected bodies at the end of the Tribulation.
    - They will be given place in the millennial reign of Christ – Rev 7:9-17.
    - They could potentially be given special duties before the Throne of God where they serve night and day – Rev 7:15.
- Church age believers will be given rewards according to their faithfulness and obedience on earth.
    - Part of that reward will be ruling and reigning over the cities during the Millennium – Matt 19:27-28; Luke 19:12-27; Rev 5:9-10; 20:4-6, 21:24, 22:5.
- God will set up an earthly kingdom with a 1,000-year reign – Rev 20:4-6.
    - Some believe the Bride of Christ (the church) will be his queen who will rule and reign with Him.
- Jerusalem will be the capital – Is 24:23, Jer 3:17, Zech 8:3.
- Gentiles and kings will come into Zion – Is 60:3-22.

- The Millennial Temple will be established (Ez 40-46). "Holy Mountain of God".
  - There is still a need for a Temple because many physical bodied people will still need to choose between worshiping God and rejecting Him.
  - This is the place provided for them to worship.
  - Everyone will make the trip to the Holy City once a year and take part in worshipping the Lord – Zech 14:16-18.
  - Those who do not make the trip will not receive moisture on their crops and they will not prosper – Zech 14:17.
- Christ will reign on earth from Jerusalem and the Millennial Temple – Jer 3:17, Is 2:3-4, Mic 4:2.
  - Sacrifices are continual (Ez 46:15), but not for atonement or a return to Mosaic Law but to remove ceremonial uncleanness and prevent defilement from polluting the Temple because the glorious presence of Yahweh will once again be dwelling on earth in the midst of a sinful and unclean people – Ez 37:28.
  - This will not be the case in the eternal state where all inhabitants are glorified and there will be no need for sacrificial purification.
- Dimensions – One square mile, which will include the outer court. It will face east – Ez 40-46.
- Theory that Temple Mount in Jerusalem is where the Garden of Eden was located, the very spot of the creation of man, place where Abraham offered Isaac, and where the Ark of the Covenant rested.
  - A river flowed out of Eden and became four heads, the Pishon, Gihon, Hiddekel (Tigris), and the Euphrates – Gen 2:10-14.
  - The head of the Gihon is a spring that comes out from underneath Temple Mount – II Chron 32:30, 33:14, Ez 47:1.
- Christ will set on the throne of David in Jerusalem and rule with a rod of iron – Rev 19:11-16, Is. 2:4, Mic 4:3..
- There is no need for the Ark of the Covenant – Jer 3:16.

Characteristics:

- No war – kingdoms will be united – Is 2:2-4.
- No crime – Jer 31:12-14.
- Animal kingdom will be at peace – predatory instincts will cease – Is 11:6-7, 65:25.
- Prosperity – no need or want, no poverty, no injustice – Jer 31:12-14, Is 25:6.
- No jealousy or envy – Is 25:11.
- Sin is kept in check – disobedience dealt with swiftly – Rev 19:11-16, Is 2:4, Mic 4:3.
- Long lifespan will return like before the Flood (Is 65:20-22), but there will be death – Is 65:20.
  - It is for the unbeliever only, absence of sickness and deformity, no disease – Is 29:18, 33:24.

- Children will be born to those physical bodied believers that go from the Tribulation into the Millennium.
    - The earth is repopulated very quickly – "nations" – Rev 20:8.
    - These children will have a choice to be saved or unsaved just like have today.
    - Many will rebel against God – Rev 20:8.
- The curse is partially lifted from the earth.
    - The full curse is lifted in the eternal state – Rev 22:3.
    - The desert will flower and become productive (Is 32:15, 35:1-2, 6; Zech 8:12), biosphere will be different, abundant rainfall in areas that are dry now.
- We may be vegetarians again. Animals become vegan which implies that humans will be as well – Is 11:7.
- Very prosperous, many advanced technologies will be discovered – Is 11:9.
- Mt. Zion will have perfect weather, no storms, floods, etc. – Is 4:5-6.
- Mist of the ground and dew will irrigate – Is 35:7.
- Harvest will be bountiful – Ez 34:27, 36:29-35; Amos 9:13-14, Joel 2:21-27.
- The nature of man will change so that he will greatly enjoy his labors (Is 65:21-23). He will be perfectly suited for the profession he has chosen.
- Time of righteousness, obedience (Jer 31:33), holiness (Is 35:8), truth (Is 65:16), and fullness of the Holy Spirit – Is 35:5.
- Living daily in the personal, physical presence of Jesus Christ – Is 30:19, 57:15; Ez 43:7; Zech 2:10-11; Rev 7:15.
- The earth will be full of the knowledge of the Lord – Is 11:9, Hab 2:14.
- Global worship of Christ – Is 2:2, 61:11, 66:18; Jer 3:17; Rev 15:4.
- No need of sun or moon – Is 60:19-20.
- Complete effects of the fall are not yet erased.
    - There will still be death – Is 65:20.
    - There will be those born who grow up and are unbelievers opposing God.
    - They will be dealt with swiftly (Rev 9:15) and some will be put to death or have their life shortened.
- There will still be one final human rebellion at the end of the Millennium – Rev 20:7-9.

Different Millennial Views

- **Post-Millennialist**
    o As more people get saved, the world will be <u>conquered</u> for Christ.
    o He will then return to set up His <u>eternal</u> Kingdom.
- **A-Millennialist**
    o There is no <u>literal</u> 1,000 years.
    o The <u>Church</u> inherits the blessing of the Promised Land.
    o Christ reigns <u>through</u> the church.
- **Pre-Millennialist**
    o Christ <u>physically</u> returns, puts down His enemies, and reigns for 1,000 years on the earth after which we move into the eternal state.
        - This is the view I believe the Bible takes because the chronological events in the book of Revelation state:
            1. <u>Second</u> Coming of Christ – Rev 19:11-16.
            2. Armageddon – Rev 19:17-19.
            3. Satan is <u>bound</u> for 1,000 years – Rev 20:1-3.
            4. <u>Final</u> rebellion – Rev 20:7-10.
            5. Great White Throne <u>Judgement</u> – Rev 20:11-15.
            6. <u>Eternal</u> state, new heaven and new earth – Rev 21:1-22:5.

NOTES:

End of the Millennium

- The complete effects of the fall are not yet erased. There will still be one <u>final</u> rebellion – Rev 20:7-9.
- Throughout the Millennium, there will be those physical bodied humans who are born and <u>reject</u> God. The number of the rebellious grows "as the sands of the sea" – Rev 20:8.
- At the end of the Millennium
    - Satan will be <u>loosed</u> from the bottomless pit – Rev 20:7.
    - He will return to <u>earth</u> for one final uprising – Rev 20:8.
    - He will deceive the nations (Rev 20:8), gather the unbelievers who are numbered as the sands of the sea, and <u>encompass</u> the Beloved City. Why? As a final proof that the heart of man is desperately wicked and can be changed only by God's grace.
    - God calls down <u>fire</u> from Heaven which devours them quickly – Rev 20:9.
- God casts Satan into The Lake of Fire where the antichrist and false prophet are <u>still</u> alive and there they will remain forever – Rev 20:10.
    - <u>Fallen</u> angels are also judged at this time – Jude v.6, II Pet 2:4.
    - <u>Christians</u> are their judges – I Cor 6:3.

Great White Throne Judgement For all <u>unsaved</u> – Rev 20:11-15.

- This event is so awful that it will not take place in heaven or <u>earth</u> – Rev 20:11.
- <u>Jesus Christ</u> is the judge – Acts 17:31, John 5:22.
    - The <u>unsaved</u> are those being judged individually – Rev 20:5, 12.
    - Believers will be <u>present</u> at this judgement but will not pass sentences.
    - As believers, we will <u>watch</u> as our friends and relatives are pronounced guilty and sent to the Lake of Fire for eternity.
- God will not wipe away all <u>tears</u> until the eternal state – Rev 21:3-4.
- Hell/Hades – Temporary holding place for those who have died <u>rejecting</u> God – Rev 20:12-13.
    - These dead come from the beginning of time until the <u>end</u> of the Millennium.
    - Some of them have been there for <u>thousands</u> of years.
    - They have already been judged guilty but are just awaiting their <u>sentencing</u>.
    - They are brought up from <u>Hell</u> for their sentencing now.
- This is the <u>second</u> resurrection – for the wicked only.
    - It is also the <u>second</u> death – Rev 21:8.
- Angels who did not keep their first <u>estate</u> (Gen 6:2) were kept in chains under darkness until this judgment – Jude 6.

Books Opened – Rev 20:12.

- **Book of Life**
    - Includes <u>names</u> of all humans who have ever lived.
    - This is God the <u>Father's</u> book – Ex 32:32-33.
    - Any human who dies without confessing Christ as Savior will have their name <u>blotted</u> out of this book by God the Father – Rev 3:5, Ex 32:32-33, Ps 69:28.
- **Another book – The Lambs Book of Life**
    - This is God the <u>Son's</u> book – Rev 13:8.
    - When you are saved, your name is written in this book, and it will never be <u>erased</u>.
- **Book of man's works and sins that will determine <u>degrees</u> of punishment.**
    - "books" <u>plural</u> – Rev 20:12, Dan 7:10
- Notice that at the Great White Throne Judgement <u>only</u> the "Book of Life" and "books" were opened. The "Lambs Book of Life" is not needed because all those who are judged are unsaved.
- <u>Jesus</u> Himself is the judge – John 5:22, Acts 17:31.
    - Just as an accountant <u>reconciles</u> his books, so will these books be reconciled.
    - Since names of the unsaved are blotted out of the Book of Life, the names in The Book of Life will be exactly the <u>same</u> as the names in The Lambs Book of Life.
- None will curse God or say He was <u>unfair</u>.
    - The <u>knowledge</u> of Christ and His sacrifice will be revealed.
    - All will <u>bow</u> before Him – Rom 14:11, Phil 2:10.
- All will <u>confess</u> that Jesus Christ is Lord – Phil 2:10-11.
- Unbelievers will not only be judged for rejecting God, which will determine where they spend eternity, but they will also be judged according to their works (Rev 20:13), which will determine the <u>degree</u> and severity of torment – Rev 20:12, Matt 11:20-24.
- If your name is not found in the Lambs Book of Life, you will be thrown into the Lake of Fire burning with fire and brimstone (Rev 20:14-15, Mal 4:1), which was <u>prepared</u> for the devil and his angels – Matt 25:41.
    - It was <u>never</u> intended for humans – Matt 25:41.
    - God made a way of salvation, but they <u>rejected</u> Him – John 14:6.
- They will possess their 5 senses, still be <u>enslaved</u> to their hang-ups, addictions, and lusts without fulfillment.
- Condition of The Lake of Fire.
    - Place of torment, thirst, thinking, no <u>escape</u> from the final sentencing.
    - Hell/Hades – place of torment, could see paradise, thirst, <u>flame</u>, fixed gulf between, concern for brothers – Luke 16:20-31.
    - It is the <u>eternal</u> abode of Satan, the antichrist, the false prophet, and all unbelieving humans – Rev 20:10.
    - This is the eternal <u>second</u> death – Rev 20:14.

After the Great White Throne Judgement

- <u>New</u> heaven and earth – Rev 21:1.
- The heaven and earth as we know it will <u>pass away</u> – Rev 21:1.
- We will enter into the <u>eternal</u> state.
    - Only those who have their name written in the Lamb's Book of Life can <u>enter</u>.
    - Only <u>believers</u> – Rev 21:27.

NOTES:

CHAPTER 12

The Eternal State

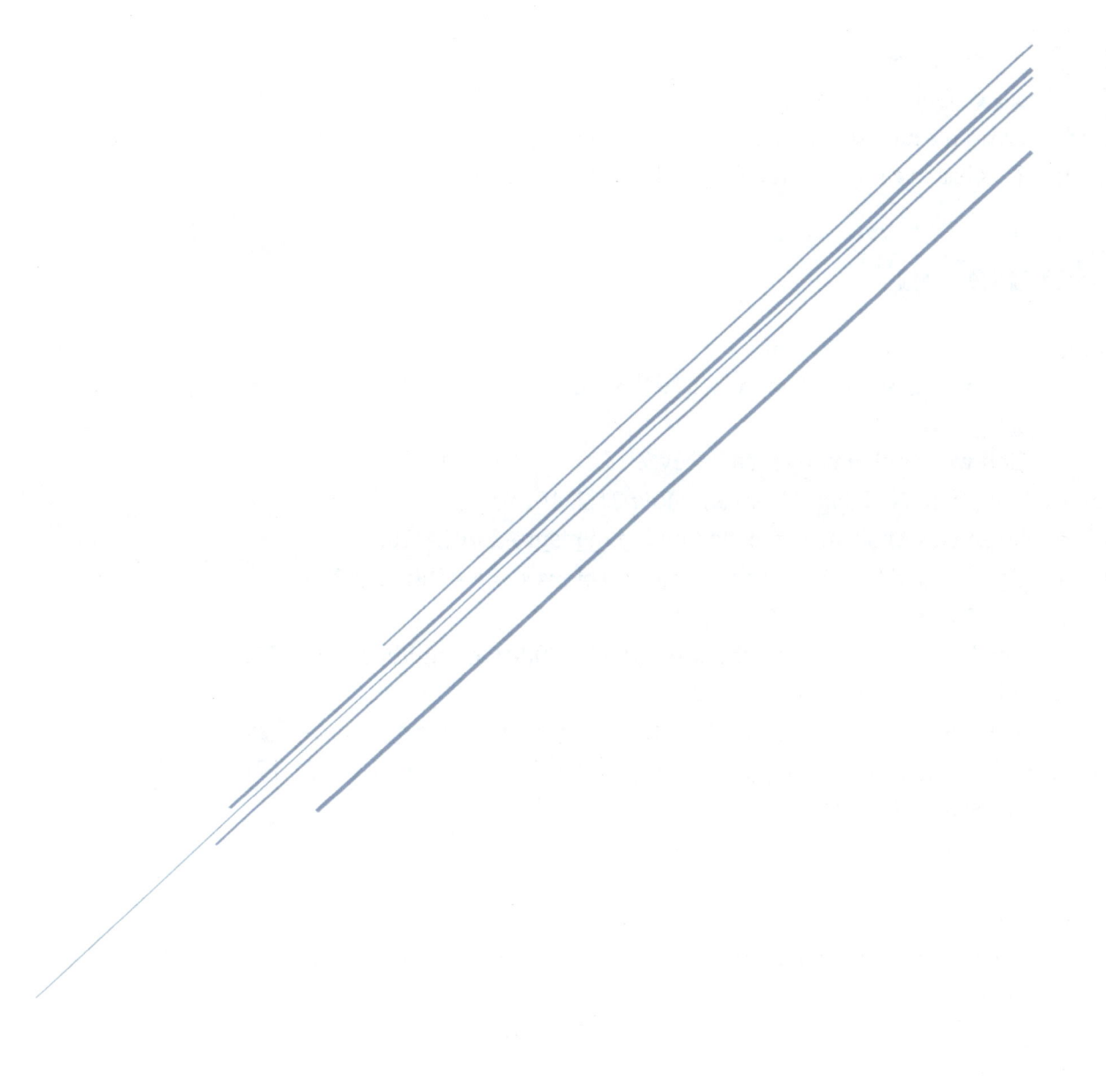

New Heaven, Earth, and Jerusalem (Rev 21:1-22:5)

- Some people believe that Revelation 21 and 22 are a <u>continued</u> description of the Millennial kingdom.
- Others believe that this is not a refurbishing of the old heaven (atmosphere) and earth but re-creating a new heaven and earth into existence – Ps 102:25-26; Is 65:17, 34:4, 51:6; Matt 24:35; Rev 21:1.
    - The old is <u>dissolved</u> by fire – II Pet 3:7, 10, 12.
- There are currently three heavens.
    1. <u>Atmospheric</u> around the earth.
    2. <u>Stellar</u> which contains the galaxies.
    3. <u>Throne</u> of God – II Cor 12:2, Rev 4-5.
- God <u>destroys</u> the atmospheric and stellar heavens and the earth.
    - This has been the abode of <u>evil</u> – Eph 2:2, 6:12.

New Jerusalem

- There is a new earthly <u>Jerusalem</u>.
    - The heavenly Jerusalem, which will no longer be in the third heaven, will have its abode on <u>earth</u> – Rev 21:2.
    - God will dwell <u>among</u> men – Rev 21:3.
- Comes down from God <u>out</u> of Heaven – Rev 21:2, 10.
    - It can be seen from a great and high <u>mountain</u> – Rev 21:10.
- Has the <u>glory</u> of God like the light of a most precious stone – Rev 21:11.
- The <u>city</u> is 1,500 cubic miles – Rev 21:16.
    - The Holy of Holies is a <u>cube</u> equal to a 74,000-floor building – Rev 21:16.
    - It is made of pure <u>gold</u> – Rev 21:18.
    - When all the atoms of gold are perfectly lined up it is <u>transparent</u> – Rev 21:18.
- Surrounded by a great and high <u>wall</u> made of Jasper, 72 yards wide (Rev 21:17) with 12 foundations of precious stone (Rev 21:19) each having a name of an apostle – Rev 21:14.
    - The wall is relatively <u>short</u> since the city is 1,500 miles high.
    - The wall is not for <u>protection</u>.
- The wall has 12 <u>gates</u> with 12 angels – Rev 21:12.
    - Each of the gates is one <u>pearl</u> (Rev 21:21) and has the names of the 12 tribes of Israel on them – Rev 21:12.
    - <u>3</u> gates on north, south, east, and west sides – Rev 21:13.

- o The original tabernacle only had one gate, <u>one</u> way in – Ex 33:9.
- o The gates never <u>shut</u> – Rev 21:25.
- o Only those whose names are written in The Lambs Book of Life have the <u>right</u> to enter – Rev 21:27.
- One <u>street</u> made of transparent gold – Rev 21:21.
- The throne of God and of the Lamb will be in the <u>city</u> and servants will serve Him – Rev 22:3.
- God and the Lamb are the Temple, no need of a <u>physical</u> temple – Rev 21:22.
- There is no sun or moon, no day or night because God will lighten it with the <u>glory</u> of the Lamb who is the light – Rev 21:23.
- No <u>remembrance</u> of the Ark of the Covenant – Jer 3:16.
- 24 <u>elders</u> crowned, enthroned, and seated around the throne of God, potentially the 12 patriarchs and the 12 apostles – Rev 19:4.
- 144,000 singing a song which no one <u>knows</u> but them – Rev 14:3-5.
  - o These are the <u>men</u> who were witnesses during the Tribulation – Rev 7:3-8.
  - o Heaven is filled with <u>music.</u>
  - o It will be a high priority, so we need to be in <u>practice</u> now.
- Pure <u>river</u> of water of life, clear as crystal, proceeding out of the throne of God and The Lamb – Ez 47:1-12, Rev 22:1, Gen 2:10-13.
  - o God will give of the fountain of the water of life <u>freely</u> – Rev 21:6, 22:17.
- <u>Tree</u> of Life – not seen since Gen 3:24 where the angels guarded it – Rev 22:2, 14.
  - o This is paradise <u>regained</u>.
  - o Has 12 manner of fruit, one for each month, and the leaves of the tree are for the healing of the <u>nations</u> – Rev 22:2.
  - o Believers have a <u>right</u> to it and can eat of it freely – Rev 22:14.
- Nations of the new earth will walk in its <u>light</u> – Rev 21:24.
- <u>Kings</u> of the new earth will bring glory and honor into it – Rev 21:24-26.
- Nothing <u>unholy</u> will enter it – Rev 21:27.
- The <u>Bride</u> of Christ is the new Jerusalem – Rev 21:9-27.
- We will have <u>access</u> to the new earth and the kings will have access to the New Jerusalem – Rev 21:25-27.

Characteristics of the Eternal State

- All things will be made <u>new</u> – Rev 21:1.
- We will see God face to face and have <u>audience</u> with Him for eternity – I Cor 13:12.
  - o His <u>name</u> will be in our foreheads – Rev 22:4.
- God will dwell <u>among</u> the people – Rev 21:3.
- Those who <u>overcome</u> will inherit all things – Rev 21:7.

- No more curse – Rev 22:3.
- No more crying, or pain – Rev 21:4.
    - Progression of pain in reverse (death, sorrow, crying, pain).
- God will wipe away all tears.
    - After the Great White Throne Judgement. It does not happen until the New Heaven and earth – Rev 21:4.
- No death, no more good-byes – Rev 21:4.
- We will not think about the old earth – Is 65:17.
- No night – Rev 21:25, 22:5.
- No sun – Rev 22:5.
- Never grow bored.
- Will sing and exalt the Name of the King of Kings forever – Ps 30:12.
- Unbroken fellowship with God, Jesus, angels, and fellow believers.
- We will serve perfectly.
    - We will have gifts and special ministry and responsibilities. There will be distinct groups with unique responsibilities.
- No seas (Rev 21:1). Seas divide people, symbolic of vulnerable humanity to the influences of Satan.
- Purified speech – one language to worship the Lord – Zeph 3:9.
- No potential for evil, no more uncleanliness, or abominations, forever removed – Rev 21:1, 27.

"Eye hath not seen, nor ear heard, neither have entered into the heart of man, the things which God hath prepared for them that love Him" – I Cor 2:9.

Response to the Knowledge

- **II Tim 4:8** – "prize (crown of righteousness) for all who eagerly look forward to His glorious return".
- **II Pet 3:11** – "Seeing then that all these things shall be dissolved, what manner of persons ought ye to be in all holy conversation and godliness?".
- **Rev 1:3** – "Blessed is he that readeth and they that hear the words of this prophecy and keep those things which are written therein: for the time is at hand".
- **Rev 22:7** – "Blessed is he that keepeth (read obediently, follow exclusively, believe totally, and study continually) the sayings of the prophecy of this book".
- **Rev 22:12** – "I come quickly, and my reward is with me to give every man according as his work shall be".
- Crowns to earn at the Bema Seat Judgement (see section on What Will Happen in Heaven During the Tribulation).

Stand Fast

- II Thess 2:15.
- Renounce sin, do not neglect church, respond to life spiritually, remain faithful.
- Ps 5:11-12 – We live behind enemy lines. Use praise as a shield.
- Eph 6:10-20 – Put on the whole armor of God.

Work Hard

- II Thess 2:16-17, Luke 19:13.
- Commit to serving and ministering, reach the lost, make disciples, build the church, use the gifts and resources the Master has given you.
- John 15 – fruit, more fruit, much fruit.

Look Up

- Anticipate His coming, be prepared, after He comes it is too late to prepare.
- Let this motivate you and be a wake-up call.
- There are rewards for those who hope and long for Christ's return.

Remember

- God still reigns – He is sovereign.
- The Church is still precious – So be faithful.
- Our mission is still clear – Be the salt and light of the world.
- Our focus is still heaven – This world is temporary.
- Our victory is still certain – I have read the back of The Book and we win.

NOTES:

References

Ankerberg, John, and Jimmy DeYoung. *Israel Under Fire: The Prophetic Chain of Events That Threatens the Middle East.* Harvest House Publishers, 2009.

Barclay, William. *The Revelation of John.* Westminster John Knox Press, 2004.

Carter, Joe. "The U.S. Sends and Receices More Christian Missionaries Than Any Other Country". *The Gospel Coalition,* 20 Feb. 2012. http://www.thegospelcoalition.org

DeYoung, Jimmy. *Revelation: A Chronology.* Shofar Communications, 2010.

Hindson, Ed. *15 Future Events That Will Shake the World.* Harvest House Publishers, 2014.

Jeramiah, David. *What in the World is Going On?* Thomas Nelson, 2008.

LaHaye, Tim, and Thomas Ice. *Charting the End Times: A Visual Guide to Understanding Bible Prophecy.* Harvest House Publishers, 2001.

Lovering, Daniel. "Missions: Most Christian Missionaries are American." *World-Wide Religious News,* 24 Feb. 2012, https://wwrn.org/articles/36949/.

Malone, Terry. "Chronological Events of the Tribulation Period." *Calvary Prophecy Project,* 20 May 2011, https://www.calvaryprophecy.com/articlesnew.html.

Naman, Ted, *Are We the Generation That Will See Christ's Return?* Printed USA, 2021.

Naman, Ted, *Revelation Through My Eyes.* Printed USA, 2014.

Naman, Ted, *The Book of Revelation Verse-By-Verse,* Printed USA, 2021.

Reagan, David R. "The Wars of the End Times." *Lamb and Lion Ministries,* https://christinprophecy.org/articles/the-wars-of-the-end-times/. Accessed 16 Feb, 2021.

The Scofield Study Bible, King James Version. (2003). Oxford University Press.

ABOUT THE AUTHOR

Sherri Lynn Reynolds was raised in Fremont, Ohio by Godly parents, Fred and Lonnie Memmer, who provided a Christian home and education. She graduated from Liberty University with a B.S. in Social Applied Psychology and is ACSI certified as a Bible Specialist. She has dedicated her life to discipleship and Christian education. She has been a youth counselor, actively participated in missions, and is currently a Christian high school teacher. Sherri has been married to her faithful and loving husband, Jim, for 23 years. She has two adult children, Ashley and Brandon, both attending college. Sherri presently resides in Oklahoma.

Made in the USA
Columbia, SC
09 January 2025